To

Mr. Miftau. Uroast

Uli BaikWihsu.

1 0 - 2 - 88

AL SAQI
BOOKS

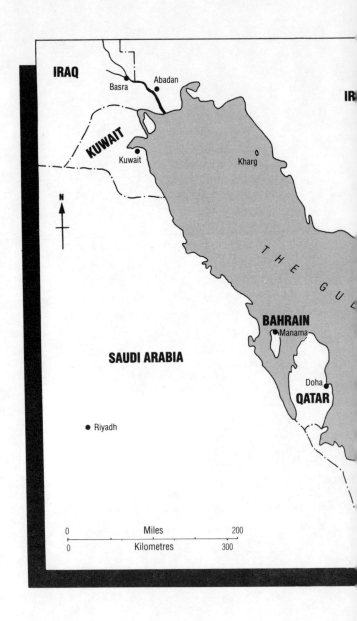

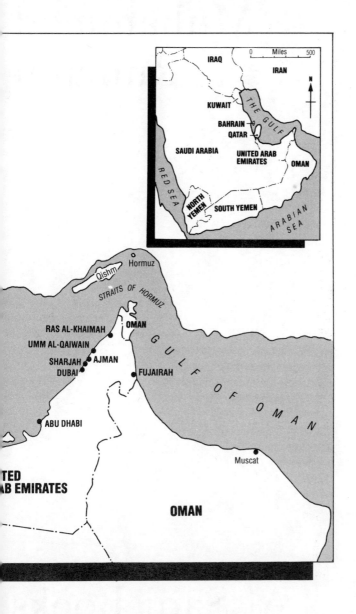

Muhammad Rumaihi

Al Saqi Books

Beyond Oil

Unity and Development
in the Gulf

Translated by James Dickins

**British Library Cataloguing
in Publication Data**

Rumaihi, Muhammed
   Beyond oil: unity and development in the gulf.
   1. Persian Gulf Region——Economic conditions
   1. Title   11. Al-Khaleej laysa naftan. *English*
   330. 953   HC415.3

   ISBN 0–86356–120–9
   ISBN 0–86356–032–6 Pbk

First published as
Al-Khaleej Laysa Naftan
by Shirka Kazhima lil-Nashr wa'l-Tarjima
   wa'l-Tawazi', Kuwait, 1983.
© Muhammad Rumaihi, 1983.

This edition first published 1986.
Al Saqi Books, 26 Westbourne Grove, London w2.
© Al Saqi Books, 1986.

Phototypeset by Cover to Cover,
Cambridge.

Printed in Great Britain by
Billing and Sons Ltd,
Worcester.

Contents

List of Tables

Preface

The Gulf is not oil. The Gulf is its people and its land. So it was before the discovery of oil, and so it will remain when the oil disappears. Oil is no more than a historical phase in this part of the Arab world—and a rather short one at that.

Few voices call attention to this fact today, and even fewer ears seem willing to listen. The people of the Gulf have grown used to living in the present, and often view the future with trepidation. It is easier to enjoy the obvious comforts of today than to take account of what tomorrow might hold.

But this unwelcome future will come upon the Gulf sooner than we might imagine if the events of the past twenty years are any guide. Between the mid-sixties and mid-eighties the region witnessed a cascade of economic, social, and political changes that would have seemed impossible only a few years earlier. This book is concerned with those changes. It deals, however, with the future and turns on two axes that are decisive for that future: namely, comprehensive development and unity.

The fate of the people and land of this region depends on real success in all aspects of development—economic, social, cultural, and political—and on the achievement of Arab unity, the hope of all the Arabs. In the case of the small Gulf states, unity is more than mere hope. Without it, there may be no future at all. Development, meanwhile, has become a prerequisite for survival, but it is inconceivable within small areas with tiny populations.

I have had some consolation for my academic efforts over the past ten years in that several of my forecasts have come true in one form or another. In an introduction to a series of lectures to students of the Arab Studies Institution in Cairo I said:

Economically, socially, and politically, the emirates are still passing through a transitional stage of development. If there is no external interference or internal impediment, the Gulf societies will eventually find themselves left with no choice but to co-operate with one another to the benefit of society as a whole in the entire region.

This was not mere speculation, but a logical assessment of the realities of the region. In the mid-seventies, at a lecture organized by the diplomatic circle of the Foreign Ministry of the United Arab Emirates I said:

Any plans for the integration of the Gulf region would involve the formation of a Central Higher Council for Energy, which would oversee oil policy in the Arabian peninsula and provide the money to finance an infrastructure through a 10 per cent levy on oil revenues to be given to a development fund for the peninsula. This council would control integrated economic policies aimed at building up communications, siting factories, training the work-force, and discovering new sources of wealth.

Some considered these proposals chimerical. But the co-operation that has already been achieved among the countries of the Gulf suggests that the ideas put forward here might also be achieved.

If co-operation has already become a fact embodied in institutions functioning in many areas, then comprehensive development and unity, which would draw the inhabitants of the region together more effectively, are also perfectly feasible goals.

It is difficult for an author to ask readers to do one thing and refrain from another. But it is my hope that this book will be seen as an integral whole. My intention is to help illuminate the way for the people of this region, and of the Arab world in general. It is certainly not to seek out mistakes and magnify them or to be excessively critical. Neither is it to distort facts, whether positively or negatively. The people of this land are human beings who sometimes make mistakes. The ideas and opinions presented in this book may sometimes be mistaken too. In any case, they are all open to discussion.

1
The Gulf Before Oil

The world today knows of the Gulf through oil. The inhabitant of the region is seen as a modern Aladdin whose magic lantern grants his every wish. The media, both local and international, tend to give the impression that life has always been a paradise in these lands and will continue to be so. Newspapers and books present a glowing, happy picture of social relations and economic life before the discovery of oil, and many prominent groups use such ideas to counteract any desire to look to the future or criticize the past.

Is the present really that wonderful for the people of the Gulf? Was the past just as splendid? Were social and economic relations as positive and uncomplicated as we are sometimes led to believe?

Pearl-Diving and Prayer

Pearl-diving was the area's most important economic activity before the discovery of oil. The Gulf had been known as a pearl-producing region since early times.[1] Pearl-diving was the prime source of income for generations.

Much of the historical information available to us dates from the emergence of modern social structures in the Gulf societies following the great migration of tribes from the interior of the Arabian peninsula to the coastal regions at the end of the eighteenth and beginning of the nineteenth century. Although we can be certain that the relations of production did not remain fixed throughout this period, the historical evidence suggests that the rhythm of economic life changed little. The pearl-diving season was roughly the summer months (from May to September), and most of the work-force was employed for no more than four or five months a year. Since few pearl-divers had any other, land-based occupation, the income of those few months had to support the pearl-diver and his family for the entire year.

We know that the beginning of the twentieth century saw a big increase in pearl-diving as an economic activity. A traveller to Kuwait during the first decade of this century wrote:

> Kuwait was also a very important centre for pearl-diving. In 1911 it had 800 boats, with around 20,000 men on them engaged in diving. These, moreover, were not natives of Kuwait, but people who had come to Kuwait from all over the region.[2]

Precise records of the distribution of investments and profit in the pearl-diving industry were kept by owners of capital and have come down to us. They show that despite the arduousness of the pearl-divers' task, and although they were the sole real producers in this kind of work, their recompense was exiguous, while the capitalists reaped great profits. Even though feudalism never existed in the Gulf in the normal sense of the word, it is legitimate to talk about 'feudalism' and 'serfdom' in this industry, for the diver became a virtual chattel of the financier and owner of the means of production.

The diving voyage, or *tarsha*, could be financed in a number of ways. The vessel might be owned by its captain, the *nukhadha*, or by a merchant. Some merchants owned more than one diving ship, and normally they also acted as *tawawish*, the buyers of the pearls at the end of the voyage. The pearls were then sold, via middlemen, on the world market in India or Europe. The ships' captains and pearl-traders constituted a small but very influential stratum. The shipowners were responsible for all the necessary preparations as regards food, drink, and the tools of the trade. Each ship carried a number of divers as well as *siyub*, or hoisters, whose job it was to bring the divers up from the sea-bed. Sometimes there was also a *radif*, or hoister's mate, and several other assistant personnel such as the cook. As far as the work itself was concerned, however, the divers and the hoisters were the most important crew-members.

The crew could be financed in various ways. One was the *salaf*, which involved a cash sum given to the diver and hoister in different proportions. This sum was normally left with the diver's family before the start of the voyage. Another method was the *taqasum*.[3] This was a payment made to the divers and hoisters over the winter period. Finally, there was the *kharjiya*, a sum given to the workers in port to spend on whatever they needed.

These monies were made available to the diver and hoister on account, and were always subject to interest set by the capitalist. The interest charged was a recognized feature of the system, and until the 'General Reform' of the pearl-diving industry in the twenties and thirties, divers and hoisters did not even have the right to know the amount of debt they had accumulated. Such debts were normally carried over from one season to the next. Payment for work was calculated according to an agreed formula. At the end of the season, after the pearl crop was sold, the shipowner—whether the captain, pearl-trader, or financier—deducted a proportion of the profits to cover the cost of water, food, and general overheads. One fifth of the remaining money—or 20 per cent of the net income— went to the shipowner. The rest was divided up into shares, called *qallata*. Each diver received three shares, as did the ship's captain. Each hoister received two shares, while the hoister's mate, if there was one on board, received one.[4]

If, for example, there were twenty divers and each received 3 shares, they would get 60 shares between them. If there were twenty-five hoisters, they would get 2 × 25, or 50, shares. Then there might be ten hoister's mates (10 shares), plus the captain, who took 3 shares. In this instance there would be 123 shares in all. The season's takings would then be divided up in these proportions.

In practice, however, matters were not so simple. The yield varied from season to season, and the diver was permanently in debt to the financier. The diving season usually ended without the diver being able to pay off the financier, let alone receive any share of the profits. The debts of the divers and hoisters tended to mount from season to season. Moreover, when a diver wanted to transfer from one employer to another, he had to obtain a certificate giving details of his debts. Finally, if the pearl-trader provided the capital for the ship, he had the automatic right to buy the catch at 20–25 per cent less than the market price, thus making even more money out of the operation.

Such were the economic relations between producer and financier in the Gulf diving industry. The ownership of the means of production was a monopoly of the merchants and financiers, who imposed a rate of interest on their capital at the beginning of the season and also held a monopoly on the sale of the produce at the end. Meanwhile the divers and hoisters lived in a state of permanent or semi-permanent indebtedness. This gave rise to a social group, or class, that might be called maritime serfs. The relationship was reflected throughout the economic and social structure of society. For the desire of the shipowners not to allow these means of production to pass out of their hands turned the mercantile and financial group into a quasi-class with its own social patterns. Thus the ship's captain held ultimate authority on board, and his influence was so great that he sometimes had the power of life and death over the divers and hoisters.

If we examine the pearl-diving legislation passed several decades ago in the Gulf, we find that it closely reflects the relations described above.[5] Article 17, for instance, states:

> If one of those participating in the dive should die and leave behind anything other than his house, it is to be divided among all his creditors, including the ship's captain, in proportion to the amount each is owed.

Article 18 states:

> If the diver dies and leaves a house but has no heir, and if the house was purchased with money from the ship's captain, it becomes the captain's property if proof of the above is forthcoming. If, however, the house was obtained through inheritance, or by some means other than pearl-diving, it is to be divided among all the man's creditors in proportion to the amount of money owed to each.

The articles of this and similar laws promulgated in Bahrain or along the Omani coast in the twenties and thirties were actually meant to lighten the burden imposed on the diver and to restore some balance in relations which were heavily biased in the financier's favour.

The relations of production on land were similarly biased in the capitalist's favour. In traditional Kuwaiti society (and the same was true of the other Gulf societies) farmers did not own the land they farmed, at least in the technical economic sense of the word. People simply had the right to exploit the land and no more.[6]

Land in the Gulf was generally owned by sheikhs who had full property rights over it, or by large landowners.[7] The rights of the agricultural worker were limited to the use of the land under conditions determined by the landowner. These were normally set on an individual basis. No general rights were enjoyed by members of the extended family unit. In certain relatively fertile regions a form of serfdom arose. The person working the land would 'pledge' a certain proportion of his produce. Such a pledge carried a high degree of risk, since it meant that the farmer had to produce at least the amount pledged in order to earn anything at all. If he failed to produce the amount promised—which happened frequently—his private property was confiscated. This practice became widespread in Bahrain,[8] where land was contracted out to farmers who pledged their produce to the landowners. Other social resources were contracted out too. In some ports the ruler would grant a merchant acting as his deputy the right to collect revenue in the ruler's name. In return the merchant undertook to pay the ruler an annual sum.[9] The merchant would set taxes on importers and others who used the port; in this way, he would recover the sum due to the ruler, while keeping any profit for himself.

Farming, practised in the oases and on the few areas of land capable of supporting seasonal agriculture, was of secondary importance compared with pearl-diving and trade. The ownership of agricultural land was based on 'tribal feudalism'. The land belonged to the sheikh of the tribe, and the farmer would have use of it in accordance with an agreed set of rules and principles.

> The ownership of land in Kuwaiti societies, as in other Arab societies, raises many problems as to whether it is a form of ownership in the technical sense of the word, or simply a form of land tenure characterized by the possession and exploitation of the land with no formal recognition of ownership by the state or society, the real owner being considered the state or the sheikh.[10]

Land ownership was vested in the ruler, or the sheikh of the leading sedentary tribe. Agricultural land either belonged to the sheikhs, or was given to leading merchants, or purchased from the latter. Land was therefore also 'pledged', since it was given to peasant families who acted as tenants and did the actual farming in return for a commitment to pay a portion of the yield, in money or in kind.

The relations of production based on individual ownership of the means of production (ships, land, wells, water, and so on) gave rise to corresponding social relations. Society was divided into a number of different interest groups. But no overt class conflict ever emerged. It was held in check by a number of factors, primarily the smallness of the society and the lack of alternatives for the majority of inhabitants, who were employed in pearl-diving, agriculture, or on merchant ships. Indeed, these were the very groups who consumed the goods transported by the merchants.

This situation was reinforced by the relative lack of social consciousness, the complete lack of any kind of education, and a widespread belief in superstition and the supernatural. Such beliefs were part of the social structure itself; they were based on the fact that pearl-diving depended on an unknown source that might yield great wealth or nothing at all. Agriculture's strict dependence on aleatory rainfall similarly fostered belief in the supernatural and a passive acceptance of fortune, good or ill.

There was a dialectical interchange between the unpredictability of men's livelihoods and their belief in superstition and the supernatural. As one would expect, the relations of production led to a comprehensive set of social relations in keeping with the economic substructure.

Social Structure and Social Relations

The tribe was the most important social group in the Gulf societies, but as tribes became anachronistic in the sedentary societies of the oases and towns of the coast, their social structure was eroded and merged into the dominant relations of production. We can thus discern the emergence of a post-tribal social structure: an extended family consisting of grandfather, father, children, and grandchildren. This itself was part of a wider tribal and kinship structure. The extended family was the unit of socio-economic production and played a central role in social regulation in traditional Gulf societies. The family owned, or rented, the means of production. The head of the family would oversee the running of a vessel or be the principal tenant of the land, and the family members would provide the workforce.

Socio-economic power was thus concentrated in the head of the household, and the traditional marriage system was strictly endogamous, so that control of the means of production would be retained. Among those who worked at sea — the majority in traditional Gulf societies — women were considered *awra*, or imperfect, and were allowed no freedom whatever, whether in choosing a husband or in expressing an opinion on the subject. As Sheikh Yusif Ibn Isa al-Qina'i put it:

> Women are considered valueless by all men except the most forward-looking. Men view them as useless chattels. If a woman is mentioned in conversation it is customary for the other person to say, 'May God honour you for mentioning her.' Young girls are forced to marry men they don't want to marry, particularly cousins, even if the man happens to be ugly and debauched. Moreover, a man of eighty might marry a girl of twenty; the girl is forced to marry by her guardian even if she doesn't want to have anything to do with the man.[11]

Writing of what he observed in the early years of the twentieth century, Stanley Mallory noted:

> If the honour of the girl is called into question, the shame can normally be expunged only by her death. There are, however, certain circumstances in which the girl is not killed, but is punished by being imprisoned in a room with all the doors and windows locked.[12]

A father's authority was absolute, extending even to the life or death of family members. Families themselves were classified as either of 'pure blood' or of 'mixed blood'. This was a division whose economic basis had disappeared but whose social aspect had been retained. There was no intermarriage between these two categories of family, even among the uppermost social stratum, for there was a taboo against relations that might lead to the disappearance of the division. Children were brought up to be blindly obedient to the head of the family, and their social upbringing stressed inflexible rules and customs.

The Legal System

These societies had no legal system in the normally accepted sense. The first laws appeared only in the second decade of the twentieth century, and dealt specifically with pearl-diving and related matters. The class character of these laws is obvious: they legalized the existing system. The pearl-diving law, drawn up in Kuwait by the ships' captains, naturally defended their interests. Article 3, for instance, stated: 'All crew members must obey the orders of the captain during the pearl-diving season both on land and at sea; they have no right to disobey his orders.'[13]

The pearl-diving courts, known as the Courts of Precedence, consisted of a panel made up of ships' captains who would judge disputes between divers and captains. They often based their judgements principally on the testimony of the captain. The traditional procedure followed in Arab courts of law derived fundamentally from the interests of the ruling class. Since this society had had no written laws, the construction of a legal system has been complicated and difficult, in particular in the present day, when new methods of production require the adoption of laws that clearly define relations between people.

One writer who has lived through this period has commented:

> From the founding of the state of Kuwait up to the present day, our judicial system has functioned in the absence of either an Islamic or a Western-style constitution, and legal judgements have been applied without demur.[14]

At the centre, authority was held by the ruler or tribal sheikh. It was then delegated to the various leaders of social units (the ruler of a bedouin tribe, the sheikh of a town), or to the ships' captains in disputes that fell within the jurisdiction of the Courts of Precedence. The authority—whether sheikh, head of a tribe, or captain of a ship—was thus able to deliver whatever legal judgements he deemed appropriate.

The Political System

The term 'political system' may be used metaphorically to refer to the political power that used to dominate the Gulf. In practice, authority was individual and operated vertically, for the ruler (the sheikh) held overall responsibility for the affairs of society. Authority was then delegated to tribal chiefs and the heads of clans and families. Amin al-Raihani provides perhaps the best description of the shift from traditional tribal authority to the centralized power of the sheikh during the formative period of the modern Gulf societies: from the middle of the eighteenth century to the discovery of oil in the twentieth. Referring to the form of political rule in Kuwait, he writes:

> Before Sabah Ibn Jabir the Second, the sheikh ruled in consultation with clan leaders. The ruler would never undertake any matter of importance without consulting them and having them consult their tribesmen. This form of consultation, however, became less important in the reign of Sabah the Second and disappeared completely in the days of Ibn Mubarak, who later ruled in his name.[15]

The same writer observes of Bahrain:

> When I was there I inquired about the form of government, and was told that there were three forms: national, foreign, and mixed. Sheikh Isa Ibn Ali administers the first; al-Bilyusi (the British agent) administers the second; and the municipal mayor al-Ajami runs the third.[16]

A study of the system of rule in traditional Gulf societies provides a clear picture of a classic transition of the division of labour from common (communal-tribal) ownership to a well-defined division of labour in the interests of one particular social group. The change from tribe to state, which took place in Gulf societies before the discovery of oil, turned the tribes themselves, in alliance with leading merchants, into instruments of political control. At first such control rested on tribal and family groups. But soon the system of tenancy became an instrument of class interests. Among the sedentary groups there were regional emirs whose authority was derived from that of the sheikh. These people would issue orders, lease land, and arbitrate disputes. The inhabitants would pay them a certain proportion of their produce.

This structure could well be described as a pre-state formation, since it relied on custom and tradition, and on a primitive oppressive apparatus. Its existence accounts for the extreme difficulties experienced by Gulf societies today in founding modern political institutions.

The Education System

Given the structure of political authority and the interests it represents, it is not surprising that political leaders took no steps to construct an education system, apart from the fact that they themselves had only a limited idea of what education was. The first seeds of an education system were planted by enlightened ships' captains and merchants, who felt that some basic form of education was necessary because of their new openness to other societies.

Traditionally, the Koran was the basis of education, and instruction consisted of reciting and memorizing holy verses. Certain *zawiyas*, as the early schools were called, also began to provide elementary instruction in arithmetic. The merchant class took the next step, raising money to establish modern schools during the twenties and thirties in Kuwait, Bahrain and Dubai, then the mercantile and maritime centres of the Gulf.[17] These initiatives met with resistance from some of the social groups who perceived education as a danger. Al-Raihani and al-Qina'i both describe the considerable resistance to modern education in the Gulf.

Certain sectors of society considered this form of education a luxury rather than a social necessity. But the principal reason for resistance lay in the changes in social structure normally brought about by education. The groups that benefited from the existing social structure wished to preserve it. Education therefore remained limited until the discovery of oil. This also explains why education has continued to lack any real content, for the rulers tend to believe that its sole purpose is to provide personnel to fill the new public offices.

Values and Customs

Values and customs are part of the social superstructure, and are therefore linked to the dominant mode of production. In areas dependent on agriculture, the palm-tree was the focal point of community life, and many customs grew up around it. The same was true of ships and the sea. Ships were associated with various folk customs, as, for instance, when a barren woman would jump onto the deck of a ship a number of times in order to conceive. There were other similar superstitions, such as the portrayal of the palm-tree as a loving mother.

The network of values and customs in pre-oil Gulf societies formed a veil that cloaked semi-feudal economic practices in the guise of piety, honesty, and trustworthiness—all of which were srongly rooted values among the working classes (farmers and pearl-divers). A similar purpose was served by belief in the supernatural: this helped explain acts of generosity and kindness on the part of the dominant groups.

The Religious System

No description of the mode and relations of production in the Gulf prior to oil would be complete without noting the influence of religion, or more accurately, of Islam. Gulf societies have members of both the Sunni and the Shi'i branches of Islam. Despite disagreements between these two branches in particular historical periods, the principles of Islam have played an important role in maintaining the social balance. Here we have an instance of a powerful element in the superstructure having had an influence on economic relations in the substructure. Many religious-minded ships' captains refused to charge pearl-divers excessive interest or to charge interest on money loaned to debtors. Similarly, religious principles—which require the believer to work towards the next life and to fear God in all his dealings—produced a psychological barrier in the minds of certain financiers and owners of the means of production, causing them to refrain from gross exploitation of those who worked for them. Moreover, because of the system of religious education, the reading of the Koran and the attempt to adhere to its precepts were adopted by many as a form of daily piety. This explains the concern with basic Islamic values shown by large sections of contemporary Gulf society.

Even before the discovery of oil, the Western imperialist powers were well aware of the economic potential of the Gulf region: they had established new relations in the area that meant they were in a position to interfere. Despite the low profits they were making from the region at the time, the imperialists saw a potential market for their products. Economic structures were modernized in order to make them compatible with the attempt to find markets.

Before the discovery of oil, these societies depended on limited economic returns and the restricted distribution of those returns. This led to social stagnation and a network of relatively inflexible social relations and values born of the semi-ossified relations of production. Although the Gulf was the commercial gateway to the whole Arabian peninsula, low income levels prevented it from developing into a dynamic and active market. The 'oil shock'—the flowering of new relations of production and the consequent change in social relations—caused, and indeed continues to cause, diverse reactions among different social groups.

2
The Gulf in History

Before the discovery of oil, was there ever a time when the Gulf region was economically integrated, however vague that concept may be? If what is meant by integration is a regional division of labour and the exchange of expertise, facilities, and services, then the answer is almost certainly 'no'. There had been economic and social relations between these societies in the past, but certainly no integration in the modern sense. The region is historically character-ized, however, by similarities in those spheres of economic activity that were both fundamental and common to all parts of this area of the Arab world.

In that sense, the Gulf is a regional unit, a coherent social and economic entity. For objective reasons, the area's social and econo-mic history became closely bound up with that of the south coast of Iran, from Abadan in the north to Bandar Abbas in the south, including the islands scattered throughout the Gulf such as Kharg (Kharij in Arabic), Qais, Zakhnuniya, Qishim, Bahrain and Das. These were all economic centres at one time or another. The Gulf's social and economic history is also bound up with both the west coast of the Indian subcontinent and the coast of West Africa. Clear signs of this contact—both material and spiritual—are still visible in the dominant culture of the Gulf today. It is therefore illogical to define a modern geopolitical area and then to use it as the basis for analysing historical relations, since the relevant geopolitical sphere has expanded and contracted over time.

Some authors have divided the economic and social history of Third World countries into two distinct phases: the era of colonial-ism and the post-colonial period. But a more complete picture must include examination of neo-colonial relations, for in many cases colonialism has assumed a guise of political innocence, apparently leaving a region and handing political control over to the local inhabitants while actually re-establishing a covert economic colonialism. The societies of the Gulf were first affected by direct, and subsequently by indirect, colonialism and they continue to suffer from various forms of the latter. It has been said that political boundaries in the Gulf were drawn in accordance with the location of oil wells, and while the claim may be exaggerated, it is not very far from the truth. It was British colonialism, and later powerful oil interests, which transformed the Gulf from the isolated outpost it had been for centuries into a sensitive and important region to which migrants flock from all corners of the earth, a region now monitored by global powers employing the full apparatus of modern science.

Before Colonialism

Before colonial penetration, the Gulf societies were characterized by a coherent social order. There were three principal social groups, two sedentary and one nomadic. The former lived in the scattered oases along the eastern edge of the Arabian peninsula, like the Buraimi oasis in Oman, or the Hasa and Jahra (Kuwait) oases. Here one sort of relatively sedentary group lived a life of virtual self-sufficiency based on its animal and agricultural produce. The other sedentary groups were in town-like settlements that grew up along the coast. Some of these have disappeared, while others—Dubai, Sharjah, Doha, Darain (in eastern Arabia, south of Kuwait; one of the biggest pearl-diving centres), Jubail and Kuwait—have flourished. The people of these large villages made their living from fishing, trade, and pearl-diving. Such villages were maritime outlets for the inhabitants of the desert and the oases. The nomadic social group was composed of the bedouin, who roamed the desert in search of water and pasture and were a population source for the relatively sedentary societies.

Movement between these three groups was quite free. The bedouin constantly moved between the coastal towns and the oases, and others travelled between the coasts and the islands in search of economic resources that could provide the basic necessities of life. There were also economic links between the three groups. The inhabitant of the mercantile coastal town, for instance, needed date produce from the oases and dried milk, oil, and wool from the bedouin. The towns provided the other groups with basic commodities secured through trade.

In the eighteenth and nineteenth centuries there were numerous migrations from the interior of the Arabian peninsula to the coastal areas. The most important of these (famous in the modern history of the Gulf) was that of the Atub (the Al Khalifah, Al Sabah, and Al Jalahma) and associated Arab tribes in the middle of the eighteenth century. There were also other well-known migrations and population shifts, such as that of the Bani Ka'b from Oman to the east of the mouth of the Shatt al-Arab in Arabistan, and the migration of the Bani Yas tribal confederation from the interior of the Arabian peninsula to the Omani coast.[1] These migrations, which sometimes resulted in permanent settlement and sometimes in further shifts, were all motivated by economic considerations. To some extent, these migrations continued into the middle of the twentieth century, though less freely and for somewhat different reasons.

Two major factors influenced the ease with which inhabitants of the Gulf could move between the coast and the islands or between the interior and the coast. First, after a treaty with the local sheikhs and princes signed in 1820, the British colonial regime in India began to penetrate the Gulf. Severe limitations on the economic activity of the region's inhabitants resulted. The British authorities deliberately fragmented the societies of eastern Arabia and Oman, sometimes through formal alliances, sometimes by hinting at military intervention, and sometimes adopting a combination of both. Imperialism also forced Arab society to turn in upon itself, as Gulf trade with India and the African coast was stifled by intense competition from the relatively modern steam-powered transportation then available to the British.

Later, trade routes between the Gulf societies themselves were cut, and they came to rely on goods transported by foreigners. The colonialists also exploited disagreements and conflicting allegiances between tribes and within single tribes, eventually turning the various areas into 'countries' and ensuring their dependence on the colonial centre. This process began in the nineteenth century and continued into the twentieth. We should note in particular the imaginary line drawn by the British across the middle of the Gulf under the 1823 agreements, which prevented Arab tribes crossing from one area to the other. Similar demarcations were later drawn between various small social groups and their neighbours, as areas were designated in which the British authorities accepted the rule of one or another tribe. A series of conflicts were thus created: they continued throughout the period of British rule and were inherited after independence by the new Gulf states in the form of overt or covert border disputes. Even today, relations among the Gulf states and between these states and neighbouring countries are marked by recurrent border disputes.[2] As a result, these areas, which had previously enjoyed a free flow of trade and people, gradually lost that flexibility, and immediately after independence there were rigid rules governing the movement of people.

The second major factor that transformed the structure and dynamic of these social formations was, of course, the discovery of oil. The first finds date back to the years between the world wars and themselves resulted from the first factor: the existence of Western power, which drew the Gulf into the world market, and imperialism's determination to sever Gulf contacts for its own advantage.[3] The discovery of oil propelled these Arab societies into the world capitalist market. Moreover, the use of technology in the production and export of oil led to development and gave rise to economic, social, and political inequalities that inhibited these societies' natural inclination towards regional unity, dragging them instead down the slope of narrow regionalism, fuelled by the production of enormous quantities of oil in some regions and the absence or retardation of production in others. The result of all this was the emergence of the city-state.

From the Rule of the British to the Rule of Oil

British hegemony was established from the middle of the nineteenth century in the Gulf, Bahrain and Qatar, and along the Indian coast. By the end of the nineteenth century it had spread to Kuwait, finally reaching Iraq by the beginning of the twentieth. A series of similar treaties—first with Oman in 1915 (particularly the coastal region of Muscat) and then with Abd al-Aziz Ibn Saud of Saudia Arabia in 1927—turned the whole region into a British protectorate. Britain was now the dominant power in the Gulf; London's hegemony was cemented by the tribal leaders, whose sovereignty over their tribes and over the lands they claimed as their own was recognized in exchange. These tribal leaders also helped Britain to maintain its vital trade corridor with minimal expenditure and effort.

The concept of sovereignty over land as understood in modern states did not originally exist in the Gulf, or at least was of little importance to the tribal leaders, the tribes themselves, or indeed even the British colonial regime. Tribes continued to migrate from one area to another, and the British view was that such migrations did no harm so long as they did not disturb the peace. People's link with the land or lack of it was determined by continued tribal allegiance and alliances between tribes. It is tribal loyalty that accounts for the creation of the present-day United Arab Emirates (UAE) and explains why neutral zones were set up between Kuwait and Iraq, Iraq and Saudi Arabia, and Saudi Arabia and Kuwait. Lands held in common by tribes that migrated between any two emirates were declared neutral zones. Certain clans from these tribes could migrate from one area to another according to economic need, while retaining their allegiance to the original tribal sheikh elsewhere. Continued common tribal allegiance in widely separated areas has, in fact, kindled boundary disputes and land claims even under the modern state. At one time, for example, Bahrain claimed al-Zubara in northern Qatar on the grounds that the inhabitants belonged to the Al Na'im tribe, who traditionally owed allegiance to the Al Khalifah, the rulers of Bahrain. At the same time, the break-up of tribal loyalties often follows disassociation from the land, as happened in the case of the migration of the Al Bu Falasah (part of the Bani Yas alliance in Abu Dhabi) to Dubai in the first third of the nineteenth century.

As British interference mounted, the colonial authorities not only prevented free movement from the south-west coast of Persia to the eastern shore of the Arabian peninsula (as in the treaty of 1823), but also began to inhibit free movement among related Arab tribal units. Under the treaty of 1869, for example, the Al Khalifah in Bahrain were forced to refrain from interfering in the affairs of Qatar, which until then had been part of the sphere of influence of the rulers of Bahrain. As another example, the lands of the powerful Mutair tribe extended from Buraida,

Unaiza, and al-Zulfa in the northern Qasim region of eastern Arabia into southern Kuwait and the neutral zones between Kuwait and Saudi Arabia, and Kuwait and Iraq.[4] This explains why members of the Mutair are now found in all the subsequently established countries in this part of the Gulf. One researcher has noted:

> Britain not only made use of agreements, the imposition of its protection, and constant military interference, but also resorted to other methods of keeping the Gulf emirates under its control and influence. It encouraged those who supported local independence and promoted the idea of power linked to specific geographical areas. Through its interference, Britain turned tribal leaders into leaders of statelets with all the trappings of the modern state, whether by drawing geographical boundaries that had previously been unknown in Arab countries or by lending a 'national' status to ships based in one or another emirate. This gave rise to the notion that the inhabitants of each emirate should have their own nationality, and customs posts were even set up. The result was the creation of emirates that were completely artificial in nature.[5]

The vital economic scope of natural social units in the eastern part of the Arabian peninsula was destroyed by Britain's random division of the land. A form of class-based regionalism, which had grown up as a result of oil, became entrenched, fostered by tribal sentiments that caused each tribe to aspire to independence from all the others.

Early on, Britain gained overall economic control over what is sometimes called the Lower Gulf, although the Upper Gulf (the area around Kuwait and Basra, in Iraq) remained under a different sphere of influence until the early twentieth century. It was the Ottoman Empire that held sway in the interior of the Arabian peninsula, particularly in Najd, and in Kuwait, al-Hasa, and Iraq. Kuwait's relations were generally with its neighbours to the north, either Basra or al-Muhammara. Human activity in this region was concentrated in the semi-circle that begins at al-Muhammara, passes through Basra, and ends in Kuwait before trailing off into the interior of the Arabian peninsula. This is not to say that there had been no economic and social relations with the Lower Gulf. But these relations were far less important than those between the societies of the semi-circle. Before the start of the twentieth century, these were two distinct economic sectors.

Thereafter, however, they began to merge, especially after the Kuwaiti-British treaty of 1899, and even more so after the First World War, when Britain assumed control of southern Iraq. In the inter-war years British authority became more firmly established, extending over the entire region. At the same time, oil began to acquire an economic dominance that matched the political hegemony of the British. The whole region was being turned into a single market, which was, however, subservient to the economy of the ruling state (Britain) and its allies. There were thus two reasons why the common economic factor,[6] which might have brought about integration, was neither spontaneous nor genuinely regional. The first was that the traditional economy was a subsistence one based on grazing and trade and creating little surplus wealth; it therefore did not allow for much regional exchange. After the discovery of oil, the economic factor also became 'common' to the whole region, while the sources of manufactured goods were associated with the oil-consuming regions. There was therefore no initial common economic factor fostering any real form of economic integration.

Had oil not been discovered in the Gulf, co-operation might have taken a different form. Economic units might have been established in some other way, with exchange arising as a result of the development of local manufacture. As it was, the existence of oil inclined multinational companies and world capitalism to continue to co-operate with the various tribal authorities. These latter also had their own personal ambitions, and the result was the entrenchment of economic dependence.

The British were concerned with one thing above all: the legitimation of tribal authority and its conversion into true sovereignty over defined geographical areas (as in the 1916 agreement with Qatar). The same was true of the Uqair negotiations, which drew the international boundary between Iraq, Saudi Arabia, and Kuwait in 1922.[7]

But although oil restricted the freedom of movement which had prevailed under the maritime, pastoral, and agricultural economy, migration was not entirely halted, particularly from areas where no oil had been found to the oil-producing regions. The establishment of states and the constant dislocation of populations forced the tribal authorities in the new states to tap human reserves of tribesmen, both in the centre of the Arabian peninsula and in the east, where the local population had social roots and links. Individuals belonging to tribes whose lands overlapped one of the modern oil states (such as Kuwait, Abu Dhabi, or Qatar) eventually attached themselves to that particular state, as, for instance, the Ajman and Mutair in Kuwait or the Murrah in Qatar. Similarly, the demands of the traditional economy (pearl-diving) had led families to drift from port to port, thereby establishing relations with other families. They later used such relations in the same way as tribal roots, attaching themselves to attractive regions.

We thus find individuals from many tribes in the various Gulf countries. There are Murrah, for instance, in Kuwait, Najd (in Saudi A.abia), Qatar, Bahrain, and the UAE. The same is true of the Ajman, Mutair, Na'im, Duwasir, Awazim, Al Bin Ali, and Qahtan, as well as other influential groups and important, or middle-ranking families. For instance, concerning the origin of a widely spread family in Kuwait, the Jina't, Lorimer writes in his famous *Gazetteer of the Persian Gulf*, 'They came from Kuwait to Bahrain'. The fact that the Mazariq (who now live in the Sabkun region of Iran) claim to be part of the Ajman tribe provides further evidence of the intermixing of populations in the Gulf and the various migrations along its shores.

Such facts led the new oil states of the Gulf to rely on tribal roots to attract new citizens. When it became clear that the population of the newly established UAE was not large enough to fulfil its ambitious development plans, the country was forced to draw on the human resources of Oman; this eventually led to a 'silent crisis' between the Sultanate of Oman and the UAE. Similarly, both Kuwait in the sixties and Qatar in the seventies added to their populations by allowing the free entry not only of specific tribes, but also of extended families with appropriate tribal roots. In the east of the Arabian peninsula, for instance, the Qataris allowed in both the Al Bu Ainain and the Khawatir (from Jubail and Dammam), as well as the Hawajir, Al Ibn Ali, and Al Bul Rumaih. In Kuwait there are families, with or without tribal roots, who used to live in Basra or Zubair. There are also groups belonging to a particular sect, such as the Shi'a of Bahrain, al-Hasa, and Kuwait, or certain groups of

Arab origin from the south coast of Iran, who came to the Gulf and settled again among their Arab kinsfolk, while retaining their local dialects. The freedom of movement and links between the various populations of the Gulf that were typical of the traditional economy have continued, albeit with restrictions, under the new oil economy. But caution in this domain has mounted as the states have grown more prosperous. Today we have what might be called 'oil regionalism', a phenomenon marked by the need to attract new immigration and the simultaneous desire to restrict it.

Results of Forced Incorporation

This 'oil regionalism' is among the most important complications in Gulf society today. Historical evidence provides incontrovertible proof of the unitary social background, great migrations, and tribal and family links in the region. Such links among members of extended families in the Gulf still exist. But the discovery of oil, the establishment of states, the requisites of regional division, the conflicts over sovereignty, the lack of economic and social consciousness among most of the people, and the emergence of a consumer society all combined to generate oil regionalism, particularly in the fifties and sixties, making it an obstacle to area-wide development and to the common utilization of resources on a regional or pan-Arab basis. So far, all attempts to achieve closer economic co-operation have encountered great difficulties as a result of this regional class sentiment, which was itself a result of the desire to establish states and the imbalanced application of imported legislation.

One of the social factors preventing economic integration in the Gulf has been the internal class structure created by the oil economies. A fairly large class of merchants arose who acted as middlemen between local consumers in the oil-producing area and Western producers. The interests of this class were linked to those of foreign companies, and they resisted any attempts to achieve closer economic co-operation among Gulf states. This was in fact a form of self-defence, particularly since it was the policy of the Western oil companies to rely on a local agent in each country, so that there were often conflicts of interest between the various agents. Moreover, these mercantile groups did not favour industrialization, and the ready availability of imports made it difficult for local goods to compete with imports. In addition, the local market was small, and real wealth was concentrated in the hands of a tiny segment of the population.[8]

The logical justification for the historical and social integration of the Gulf is the view that this region is part of a much larger unit, the Arab nation. Many of the social and historical characteristics of the Gulf are shared by other countries of the Arab world. The Gulf societies long suffered from political fragmentation and direct colonialism. Subsequently, most of them were forcibly incorporated into the capitalist economic system. Some, in an attempt to break free of this system, adopted alternative economic plans in an effort to achieve self-reliance. But the countries of the region, which depend on a single basic resource (oil), are able to operate only within the context of the world market. Their trade and links with the world market are more important than their trade and links with each other, both because of the nature of the product and because of their luxury-orientated consumer policies.

Moreover, because of the relative (or even complete) lack of economic infrastructure capable of production, the absence of any real desire to set up productive industries, and the small size of the local market (a result of the various factors we have mentioned and the social structure of the oil states, in turn generated by this kind of economy), the majority of these states spend most of their enormous income from oil revenues on recurrent expenditure, and little on recoverable capital expenditure. One study[9] of oil revenues and expenditure in the Gulf states between 1950 and 1970 noted that in Bahrain as much as 96 per cent of oil revenues went to cover current expenditure, while the figure was 90 per cent in Kuwait. Another study showed that 99 per cent of oil revenues was set aside for the ruling family in Bahrain and 82 per cent in Kuwait. The study commented that similarly high ratios were found in the other oil emirates (Qatar and Abu Dhabi). It concluded that the factors determining the division of oil revenue are traditional and political rather than specifically economic.

It therefore seems clear that there will be no progress towards real economic integration until these countries take the political decision to adopt common economic and social policies. The form of such integration would, of course, have to be defined by the human and economic realities of these countries.

There are clear social and historical bases for this proposed economic integration. There have been long extensive human contacts, and the common culture is striking. Kuwaiti songs, for instance, are requested by listeners to Radio Baghdad just as often as they are in Sharjah. Both the daily and the weekly press constantly talk of the 'Gulf man'. But little more than songs and talk will be forthcoming unless the people are convinced that they have common economic interests, just as they have common family and cultural ties. It is to this economic question that we must now turn.

3
Development:
Why and How?

In medieval days alchemists sought the philosopher's stone that would turn base metals into gold. The goal of this and similar endeavours was always the same: to create great wealth with little expenditure of effort. More than a few people seem to believe that the alchemists' efforts have finally borne fruit in the Arab oil area. Here is a black gold that has made a poor land rich and perpetually prosperous.

The basic outline of events is clear. Oil was discovered in some countries of the Arabian peninsula, bringing vast revenues with it. These revenues were spent on the infrastructure and on services of all sorts, from roads and ports to schools, universities, and clinics. A certain portion of the inhabitants of this society ceased to live in shacks and mud-brick houses in the barren lands near the coast or in the depths of the desert and moved into air-conditioned houses in suburban areas enjoying a full range of services.

But beneath these superficial developments, important questions have begun to confound an ever-increasing number of the inhabitants of the oil-producing countries of the peninsula. Only one generation ago the Gulf countries[1] formed a little world of their own, bounded by the desert. People lived simple lives based on an economy close to subsistence, in which a tiny surplus satisfied the limited needs of a small number of people. The majority of the population, accepting their fate with equanimity, worked at sea, in the feeble agricultural sector, or as camel and livestock herders. Although working conditions were harsh, they were none the less considered natural by most people at the time.

Then oil burst upon this small world and inundated it with sudden wealth and the fruits of Western civilization, hurling it into the heart of the world economy. The transformation inevitably gave rise to profound social, economic, and political challenges. The most serious challenge was posed by a simple but crucial question that has yet to be answered: Where do we go from here? Or in other words: Will the Gulf return to the hard times of the past, or is there a way forward towards new horizons in a post-oil era?

There are those who view the future with despair, recalling the boom towns of the American gold rush that later turned into ghost towns. Oil has been compared to the gold wealth of imperial Spain after the colonization of Central and South America, when ton after ton of gold was shipped home, and soon squandered on luxury consumption. Other comparisons have been made too: Peru enjoyed a period of sudden prosperity when guano, used as a fertilizer, was discovered in the middle of the nineteenth century; Brazil enjoyed temporary prosperity with the discovery of the rubber tree. There is no lack of historical examples of a sudden prosperity that impedes long-term economic growth and stifles cultural progress.

Those who hold this point of view argue that the oil era in the Arabian peninsula is a time of sudden but fleeting prosperity that will excite the highest hopes and arouse the greatest jealousy and hatred but will come to nothing in the end, because none of the pre-conditions for comprehensive development exist.[2]

Others adopt a different attitude. History, they say, does not repeat itself. Today we have the intelligence and the planning ability to convert sudden prosperity into true economic development; in fact, a great deal has already been done. In this view:

> It is our aversion to all forms of immodesty that prevents us describing a particular university as the biggest in the world, or a particular factory as the biggest in the Middle East. Such aversion has its justifications. It must not, however, lead us to the opposite extreme and cause us to deny the importance of what we do produce, or to portray our achievements—which are genuine and practical achievements—as less significant than they really are.[3]

Between these extremes of optimism and pessimism lies a wide range of confusion, and of awareness of the historical crisis.

The new awareness about economic life in the oil countries of the

Arabian peninsula centres on two important facts. First, today's economic prosperity rests on a single commodity. Quite apart from any debate about policies for the use and distribution of oil revenues, the inescapable fact of the matter is that every barrel of oil extracted reduces the number of barrels left to be produced in the future. In other words, the economy is founded on an exhaustible base, one that, unlike agriculture or industry, cannot be regenerated. Any oil revenues that do not go towards new productive investment are irrevocably lost to future generations. If these exhaustible resources are not converted into new resources, then prosperity will simply disappear.

Second, most expenditure in the oil-producing countries of the Arabian peninsula, whether capital or current, is totally dependent on oil revenues, as is shown by the figures in Table 1. In 1979 oil constituted more than 90 per cent of the export income of the oil-producing countries of the Arabian peninsula. To make a comparison with other developing countries: as of 1972 there were forty-one non-oil-producing countries whose economies were dependent on a single commodity, the average degree of dependence on that commodity for export revenues being 50.7 per cent. Obviously, any fluctuation in export levels or oil revenues would have dangerous consequences for the general economic situation.

These two complementary facts lead us on to the concept of 'development' as understood by most modern theoreticians. The traditional concept was based mainly on average *per capita* income in a given society, supplemented by a number of other indicators, such as the number of hospitals, kilometres of metalled road, the infant mortality rate, and so on. This definition, however, does not take account of the special characteristics of the socio-economic structure of the oil-producing countries of the Gulf.

More recent development theories pay greater attention to the potential within a society for, first, increasing the productivity of the individual and, second, enhancing that society's ability to bring about a planned increase in the production of goods and services. This view presupposes the existence of a productive base which is to be developed and whose products are to be equitably distributed.

The peculiar features of the problem of development in the Gulf countries, however, render these conceptions moot. Many analysts of Gulf development have failed to realize both the extent to which a

Table 1: The Oil-Exporting Countries

	Oil exports as a proportion of all exports		Oil exports as a proportion of total local production		Oil products as a proportion of total local production	Oil revenue as a proportion of government revenues
	1974	1979	1974	1979	1979	1979
Saudi Arabia	99.7	99.8	79.1	59.9	62.2	91.2[2]
Kuwait	96.9	94.5	78.7	76.0	72.1	81.8[2]
United Arab Emirates	98.7	94.3	85.0	68.6	69.5	95.7
Qatar	98.2	94.9	87.4	77.4	79.0	93.7
Oman[1]	99.9	89.6	70.3	63.7	63.8	85.7
Bahrain	32.1	31.2	29.2	—	32.8[3]	77.0
Primary resources other than oil	45.4	50.7[3]	18.0	17.1[3]		

Source: International Monetary Fund, Global Financial Statistics. Reports and Estimates of the Committee of the International Monetary Fund.

Notes: 1. Net oil exports.
2. 1979–80.
3. 1978. Ratio of the single basic export to total local production.

productive base is lacking and the truly feeble state of renewable, non-exhaustible, locally generated capacity. Oil itself has been uncritically taken as a productive base and source of renewable productive capacity, and this has caused economists to forget about agriculture and industry.

The type of development required in the oil-producing countries of the Arabian peninsula today must aim at effecting changes in the socio-economic structure so that it becomes capable of generating a self-supporting productive capacity that can lead to a planned increase in real average income in the foreseeable future.[4] A 'renewable' and self-sustaining productive base is the primary requisite. This may appear relatively simple, since the oil revenues are collected by governments, and the latter are therefore able to finance investments, and to convert revenues into new resources, without passing through the grinder to which Third World states that have not been blessed with this bounty are subjected: arduous taxes, pressures and incentives on the local population to save, the humiliation and dependence of foreign debts.

In fact, however, the process is not nearly as simple as it may appear, for there are both objective and subjective obstacles to the establishment of this new, self-supporting productive base. These may be classified under six headings, three subjective and three objective. The former are: the nature of the society and composition of the population; the character of oil revenues; the absorption capacities of the Gulf countries. The objective factors involve serious structural weaknesses in the areas of: labour-power and effective education; expertise and administrative organization; food sufficiency and regional security.

The Nature of the Society and Composition of the Population
Most theoretical works on Third World development quite rightly discuss the link between the centre and the periphery, which leads to the transformation of production in the Third World from pre-capitalist or traditional modes to a dependent form of capitalism. The latter normally comes to predominate over the former and provides the link to the world market. In such societies, however, the traditional form of production that prevailed before capitalist penetration retains some influence over the overall social structure and continues to play a role in shaping the superstructure. An

analysis of the traditional forms of production helps to illuminate the new social formation.[5]

The peculiar characteristic of the oil-producing countries of the Gulf, however, is that the modern economic sector has entirely replaced the previously dominant modes of production, so that there is now no division between traditional and modern economic sectors. The lack of this duality, combined with the character of the new oil income, paradoxically reinforced patriarchal tribal relations. Oil revenues were (and still are) the public property of the whole society, until entering the public treasury. Thereafter they were channelled into local development projects that were totally dependent on government decisions, which were in turn dependent on the interplay of social forces at the local level.

The tribal and family formations into which these oil revenues poured were governed by traditional dominant values and relations so entrenched that for a long time they determined how this revenue would be spent. At first the idea was to distribute it in three main ways: as public expenditure, as stipends to the ruling family, and as funds for the public reserve. In some states this division has now ceased. But the fact remains that distribution and expenditure policies have been subject to great local and external pressures.

Human considerations, social relations, and the general nature of the social structure, born of the previously dominant mode of production, played a major role in determining how oil revenues were spent. The unwritten rule was that the government should attempt to provide the highest possible personal incomes, whether through direct aid (government housing, road-building, the establishment of schools and hospitals, provision of employment, the guarantee of medical treatment abroad) or through indirect contributions such as the purchase of former estates at uneconomic prices, maintenance of a monopoly on the import and distribution of goods and services, and the water supply. General and current expenditure have therefore consumed most of the oil revenues. These policies stimulated the demand for services, and the population's attitude shifted from accepting these services to demanding more of them.

Such policies were possible because of steadily rising world demand for oil and the ever-higher prices being paid for it. With the fall in demand and prices, and the attempt to create an alternative economic base (whether internal or external), the policies were soon found to be wanting. The continued practice of providing virtually free services, as well as the emergence of pressure groups that swiftly attained political influence, were among the most important factors preventing an emphasis on purely economic questions as opposed to human and social considerations.

The Character of Oil Revenues

The ease with which oil revenues can be raised has helped to determine the nature of government and personal expenditure. Just after the oil price 'explosion' of 1973, the cost of public and private projects seemed unimportant, and indeed was largely ignored. Citizens and foreign residents alike had become accustomed to high rates of inflation, while the fact that oil would ultimately run out was treated as a kind of fantasy. The belief in automatic and continual growth went entirely unquestioned, and those who demanded planned growth were virtually ignored. The constant leap in oil prices in the seventies gave rise to the slogan 'Wine today, and work tomorrow' while the buoyant oil market and galloping development fuelled unproductive public expenditure and luxury private consumption.

The notion of the value of work and production ceased to be of any great importance for the people of the Gulf. Instant wealth became an end in itself. Moreover, economic growth was not accompanied by a just distribution of its fruits, and this worsened social problems. Even more important, the flood of oil money served to tie these societies even more closely to the productive activities of the West.

The sudden influx of oil revenues thus became an obstacle to the establishment of a genuine productive base, stifling any spirit of competition and initiative, depriving the people of any incentives, and increasing dependence on Western production.

The Absorption Capacities of the Gulf Countries

The challenge of converting a proportion of oil revenues into an alternative productive base necessarily raises questions about agriculture and industry as bases for internal growth. In the case of agriculture, there are a number of genuine obstacles.

The small amount of land capable of sustaining agriculture, the shortage of water, and the low number of people willing and qualified to work in this field are serious objective impediments to the development of alternative internal economic resources through agriculture. Despite a few successful projects, various factors relating to the work-force and to economic returns have hampered agricultural development even in Oman, with its relative abundance of water. The high cost of production and lack of a trained work-force have undermined those projects that do get started.

Greater hopes have been pinned on industry, where big projects have been launched or are planned for the future.[6] These schemes have enthusiastic supporters:

> It is impossible to transfer technology or to develop the work-force in a vacuum. Suitable means must be found to encourage these processes. Industry is one of the most successful methods of transferring expertise and developing the national work-force.[7]

It is also possible to look at industry as a means of converting oil wealth into technology. Saudi Arabia's oil minister, Sheikh Yamani, has commented:

> In order to stimulate development, we have arrived at a formula whereby foreign investors with experience and technology are encouraged, through oil, to involve themselves as partners in industrial projects. They are thus given the option of buying 500 barrels of oil a day at Saudi government prices for every million dollars they invest in these projects. The number of barrels of oil exchanged in this manner has now reached about a million a day.[8]

But there are problems in building up an alternative economic base through industry. The construction of factories in these countries, for instance, has proved relatively expensive. In the early seventies the cost of building petrochemical factories in the region was two to three times higher than in Europe or Japan. Even in the eighties the cost of building some factories in the region is about 50 per cent higher than in Europe or Japan.[9] As the Saudi minister of industry has pointed out:

We are an area of low population density and limited markets. Moreover, we lack experience in the field of industry, and for the past few years have been suffering from the pressures of very high inflation.[10]

Nevertheless, industry remains the best bet, and the same minister also noted:

The hydrocarbon industries which we will be establishing depend on a limited work-force and will be orientated primarily towards world markets; moreover, the beast of inflation has been largely tamed, so that there is no longer any justification for the doubts raised, whether deliberately or not, about efforts at industrialization in the Gulf.[11]

Questions about the feasibility of establishing a productive base through industrialization are legitimate. The small size of the trained local industrial work-force, widespread reliance on foreign labour, the direct and indirect support that must be given by the state, and the relatively low returns on capital invested in industry compared with commercial banking are the main problems.[12]

External investment has also been suggested as a means of converting oil revenues into productive bases. After the 1973 price rises, these revenues flowed in at a much faster rate than the Gulf economies could absorb. A phenomenon unprecedented in economic history thus arose: the association of underdevelopment with the removal of capital abroad. Investment was concentrated in the European and North American money markets. Oil money remained in the form of deposits and investments in financial portfolios, treasury and government bonds, and shares in foreign companies. This was considered relatively more secure than direct investment. Certain economists attributed this tendency to the nature of Gulf investors, who found it fairly easy to invest in real estate and mercantile ventures.[13] However, the relative lack of alternative investment opportunities provides a perfectly adequate explanation for such actions, which were intended to maximize returns by diversifying money in bank deposits, real estate, shares, bonds, and currencies on the world market. Though some Gulf countries displayed greater wisdom than others, the management of foreign assets was until recently subject to a single central authority that displayed little dynamism and wasted great opportunities.[14]

Foreign assets belonging to the governments of the six Gulf oil-producing states were estimated in 1981 at a total of $256 billion. This capital was invested in Europe and America. But studies show that these countries:

> generally place excessive emphasis on short-term investments as well as loans and other financial transactions, because of the importance of achieving a high average return as an alternative to oil revenues, which are now in decline.[15]

Despite the relative success enjoyed by some foreign investment, there remain two fundamental obstacles to complete success: the weakness of the local investment apparatus (and lack of experts and other personnel) and, more important, the harsh anti-investment laws in the countries in which the investments are located. Such laws could at any moment pose a dire threat to the very basis of the investments themselves.

The objective obstacles are formidable too.

Labour-Power and Effective Education

Demographic statistics tell us that if foreign workers continue to migrate to the Gulf at present levels, the proportion of local inhabitants will constitute only 5 per cent of the total population by the end of the century.[16] (See Ch. 9 for a more detailed analysis.) The fundamental demographic characteristics of the Gulf countries are the small size of their populations and the high rate of immigration, both Arab and non-Arab. There is already a large foreign population, now estimated to be the majority in three countries, whereas in the mid-seventies the local population was about three-quarters of the total. Proportions vary widely from country to country. The local population is nearly 80 per cent of the total in Oman, Saudi Arabia, and Bahrain, slightly under half in Kuwait, and about a third or less in Qatar and the UAE.[17]

There is a link between the various population groups and the elements of the work-force. Taking all six countries as a whole, citizens constituted slightly more than half the work-force in the mid-seventies; in individual countries this proportion varied from about two-thirds in Saudi Arabia and Bahrain to less than half in Oman, and less than 15 per cent in the UAE and Qatar.

By the beginning of the eighties, citizens made up only 41 per cent of the total population in Kuwait, whereas the figure had remained at about 47 per cent between 1960 and 1975. There was a similar change in Bahrain—from a situation where the citizenry constituted the majority of the work-force to one in which they were a minority. In the UAE the percentage of the work-force made up by citizens fell to slightly less than 10. In some cases the immigrant labour is not even Arab. In Abu Dhabi, for example, 42 per cent of government employees in 1982 were Asians.

In practice this structural imbalance prevents the establishment of an industrial base, since that would lead to an even greater need to import foreign workers and consequently to stronger economic, social, and political pressures.

At the same time, the education systems are markedly failing to provide personnel to fill even the relative gaps in some professions (particularly technical ones), since most local students are oriented towards higher education, and to the humanities in particular.

The foreign work-force in the Gulf can be divided into Arabs mainly from countries near the Arabian peninsula (principally Egypt, Jordan, Palestine, Syria, and Lebanon) and workers from the Indian subcontinent or South-East Asia.

The current composition of the work-force leads to four major problems: an almost complete dependency on imported labour; a general rise in concealed unemployment among local and foreign workers alike; a marginalization of the national work-force; the adoption of labour-intensive production methods.

Expertise and Administrative Organization
The sudden influx of oil revenues led to an enormous rise in expectations among the local population and to the establishment of new institutions, economic structures, and services, all of which required a complex administrative apparatus. A labour-force trained in modern administrative methods was needed for public, mixed, and private management. This gave rise to what has been called the administrative vacuum.[18]

The various governments took on most of the responsibility and are now in charge of virtually everything from the planning and scheduling of public budgets to the implementation of industrial, social, and service projects (although the private sector may sometimes take over some of the administrative tasks in mixed projects). The over-extended government apparatus has all but collapsed under the burden.

The shortcomings of the local work-force were an important factor affecting the choice and implementation of development programmes, just as the future reserves and training of this local work-force will continue to be the basic factor determining the form of development and growth in these countries.[19]

Even though more than a quarter of a century has passed since the first steps to growth were taken, education programmes, for example, are still unrelated to the real needs of development in any of the Gulf countries. No effective administrative leadership was ever created, and this has led, at the very least, to a failure to keep up with developments and to provide new information and any real understanding of contemporary management practices. Organizational structures, procedures, systems, regulations, and management methods have scarcely been modified and have therefore been unable to adapt to new responsibilities. At the same time, the policy of guaranteeing citizens government jobs has led to an artificial expansion of the administrative apparatus, duplication of duties, and a vagueness about where responsibility lies. The result has been the emergence of what has been termed the 'bedouinocracy'. Lack of administrative cohesion has made it impossible to fulfil schedules. Moreover, the choice and promotion of officials continue to depend on social factors rather than objective standards. The result is low productivity and a weak incentive system.[20]

Food Sufficiency and Regional Security
One of the greatest problems of the Gulf countries is their dependence on imports for virtually all technological and even food needs. Although some of these imports are non-essential, foreign food will always be vital. Granted, there are a few pockets of farming and some land is capable of supporting agriculture in Saudi Arabia, on the coast of Oman, and in some other areas. But although a number of studies are optimistic that these agricultural experiments will yield widespread benefits, it remains the case that the oil-exporting

Gulf countries still depend on imports for their basic foodstuffs.

The rise in population has brought even greater reliance on food imports. Most, if not all, meat, cereals, and fruit are imported. Local production can match consumption only for limited periods. Fish stocks in the Gulf have been depleted by a combination of maritime pollution and widespread use of modern fishing methods.

If food security is an obstacle to growth, security in the normal sense of the word is an even greater one. The early eighties saw sweeping changes in neighbouring countries. The two principal upheavals were the Iranian revolution and the ensuing Iran-Iraq war, in which the oil countries of the Gulf soon became involved as suppliers of military aid to Iraq. Internal social changes have given rise to new political aspirations that cannot be ignored.

Expenditure on arms and the establishment and training of sizeable military forces have therefore begun to consume a fair proportion of the income of the Gulf countries. It has also increased their links with various Western powers. This has sharpened East-West conflict in the region.

Because of their reliance on oil, a non-renewable resource subject to world price fluctuations, the Gulf countries show annual budgets with surpluses and deficits over which they have little control. Moreover, the profound structural weaknesses in the human base, the lack of alternative sources of wealth, the relatively recent stage at which these societies embarked on development, and the six objective and subjective factors discussed above have all combined to generate a whole set of other dynamics, some of which accelerate growth and some of which impede it.

The problems facing these societies are not easy. A number of experts in the field have suggested that development difficulties could be attenuated by regional integration. This would help to solve the problems of underpopulation and might generate new sources of wealth, as well as creating a larger market.

From the Union of Nine to the Union of Seven

By the time the Gulf emirates achieved independence from Britain in 1971 (following Kuwait, in 1961), about a century had passed since the opening of official relations with Britain, and unofficial relations had existed for much longer than that. Sir Geoffrey Arthur, the last British official resident in the Gulf, noted after independence:

> When Britain attempted to look up all the treaties and alliances binding it to the Gulf emirates, it proved impossible to produce a comprehensive list. Therefore, when Britain undertook to agree to independence, it made do with the stipulation that all prior treaties were to be annulled, without listing them.[1]

This provides an indication of just how long and complicated were the relations between Britain and this part of the Arab world.

Legal analysts disagree about the nature of the ties between the emirates and the British authorities, and about whether relations existed with the Bombay government (the British regime in India) or with London directly. Some argue that the Gulf countries were protectorates, and claim that legal sovereignty was never altogether relinquished.[2] One commentator who accepts this point of view goes so far as to say:

> The system whereby the Gulf became a protectorate was not imposed. Rather, it developed internally and was strengthened by the request of the rulers of the emirates themselves that it be continued and maintained as a means of preserving the existence of the entities concerned, over which Britain had recognized the sovereignty of the local rulers.[3]

There can be no doubt that this view is utterly naive, for in the negotiations leading to independence Britain maintained that previous treaties had been signed by the forefathers of today's emirs in their capacity as tribal leaders, and not as heads of states.[4]

In fact, Britain's role had been divisive throughout. Until the late eighteenth century, there had been only two political entities in this region of the Gulf: Oman and the area known historically as Bahrain. Indeed, at certain periods of history, they were both parts of a single political unit.[5] The modern era has seen a revival of the idea of Oman and the Gulf, as evidenced in the literature of the national movements, which have called for reunification of the Gulf on the basis of these historical precedents. Unification is therefore not a new notion. But the political structures that have arisen in the modern era since the period of British colonial rule are quite new.

Britain promoted the fragmentation of the Omani Empire in the nineteenth century, encouraging, for instance, the secession of Zanzibar from Oman in 1860 and splitting Bahrain off from Qatar in 1868. Similarly, it separated Dubai from Abu Dhabi in 1839 and Ras al-Khaimah from Sharjah in 1921.

New tribal alliances appeared on the Gulf scene in the late eighteenth century after the decline of the Persian Empire and the collapse of Portuguese power. But Britain prevented them from playing any important role in the region, exploiting tribal disagreements to block the formation of larger regional units.

By the second half of the eighteenth century, five principal political powers had emerged in the eastern Arabian peninsula: first, the Atub alliance,[6] which led to the emergence of the Al Sabah, present rulers of Kuwait, and the Al Khalifah, present rulers of Bahrain; second, the Qawasim alliance; and third, the Bani Yas alliance. (These all played a part in the recent emergence of the UAE.) The other two powers were the Wahhabi state (later Saudi Arabia) which arose in the middle of the Arabian peninsula and the Al Sa'id state in Oman.

In the last quarter of the nineteenth century and the first quarter of the twentieth European rivalry over the Gulf sharpened. Britain moved to sign further treaties with the Gulf sheikhs in the 1880s, principally to prevent them from entertaining relations with outside powers or from mortgaging or leasing any part of their territories to foreign powers other than Britain. These 'Prohibition Agreements'[7] mark the point at which the British government first began to represent the emirates internationally. They were later prohibited from taking any action whatever without the agreement of the British.[8]

Britain derived its greatest benefit from these agreements after the First World War, when the Gulf virtually became an uncontested British lake. In the early years of the twentieth century, Britain had consolidated its internal influence by issuing the Orders of the King's Council, which empowered British political agents in the emirates to take charge of legal disputes involving foreigners and to try them in their own private courts. These courts were granted sole jurisdiction even if one of the parties to the dispute was a local citizen.[9]

When these orders were first applied in Bahrain in the early 1920s, they gave rise to a dispute over a question of particular relevance to our discussion: was an Arab from one of the neighbouring Gulf countries a foreigner or not? The question was raised by Sheikh Isa Ibn Ali, ruler of Bahrain from 1869 to 1923. The British authorities replied that anyone who was the subject of another emirate was a foreigner.[10] Subsequently, when Abd al-Aziz Ibn Saud founded the third Saudi state (1902–32), Britain began to perceive his ambitions as a threat to their hold on the Gulf, despite his protestations of friendship. They therefore signed two treaties with him in 1915 and 1927, which stipulated that he should not interfere in the internal affairs of the Gulf emirates. Then, at the Uqair conference of 1922, the British opened negotiations over the Saudi-Kuwaiti borders on behalf of Kuwait.

The British authorities also tried to prevent the emergence or expansion of new emirates and to do away with existing ones, depending on where their interests lay. In 1871 they encouraged an increase in the area belonging to the Abu Dhabi emirate in an effort to block Turkish expansionism.[11] In the nineteenth century they prevented the Al Jalahma—the third element in the Atub alliance —from setting up their own 'entity' in any of the Gulf regions, because the Al Jalahma were considered anti-British. They took similar action against the Kibsa tribe when it tried to occupy the area between Qatar and Abu Dhabi. Much later, when Britain was seeking a stop-over point for its aircraft on the way to India, opposition was encountered from the Gulf emirs. It therefore persuaded the ruler of Kalba, who owed allegiance to the emir of Sharjah, to set himself up as an independent sheikh. He thus gained the right to a military salute in return for granting British aircraft permission to land in Kalba. Thus did the emirate of Kalba come into existence in 1936, only to vanish again in 1952, when Britain had ceased to derive any advantage from it.

Britain exploited the historical legacy of the region to bolster its own interests, whether through the protection of foreigners, the appointment of emirs who would sign oil agreements on favourable terms, or the proclamation that the region was officially under British protection and influence. Between the two world wars, the British government, as part of its general stance against any advance of unity on Arab soil, stood against unity in this region as well.[12]

Conflict Between Brothers

Tribal disputes, whether between different tribes or rival groups within a single tribe, helped the British consolidate complete control of the Gulf region and afforded them the opportunity to fragment it. The worst conflicts of this kind were those between members of the same family driven by a thirst for power. Throughout the nineteenth century and a great part of the twentieth the history of power struggle in the Gulf is one of assassination and counter-assassination. As Amin al-Raihani aptly put it:

> The usual reason for this kind of dispute, common within the families of Arab emirs, was the polygamous marriage system, which gave rise to long-running feuds between blood brothers and conflict between mothers, particularly if they were of different tribes.[13]

This atmosphere of conflict and rivalry between ruling families and within single families is a real factor in the structure of political power even now, although it has been less obvious since the Second World War. One particular result of the situation, however, is still quite evident: the privileged position of the ruling family within each emirate. It is the family that sustains the ruler, particularly through the financial and political privileges created by oil money. Some political analysts argue that the Gulf family can be said to constitute a party in the modern political sense. A number of ruling families have taken steps to expand their own 'party-family', either by encouraging intermarriage or by incorporating into the tiny ruling clique other families that may perhaps be only distantly related. The party-family is in turn sustained by deep-rooted patriarchal relations that sanction its rule. The positive side to this system is that it concentrates power, but its effect on state-building has been negative. Similarly, the lack of any institutionalized method of transferring power in some emirates (explicitly confirmed in several of the modern constitutions) has opened the way to the emergence of dangerous rivalries during any change-over from one ruler to another.

Economic and Social Structure

The economic activities of the various Gulf emirates were strikingly similar up to the early years of the twentieth century. Small-scale agriculture in the oases and around water sources, widespread pastoralism in the lands of the interior, and pearling in the large villages of the coast (the basis of a lucrative trade for ports like Kuwait, Bahrain, and Abu Dhabi, particularly at the end of the nineteenth century and the beginning of the twentieth) were the backbone of the economy. Trade between the various Gulf ports, which acted as gateways to the coasts of India and East Africa, was also significant. The economy was unable to support any real capitalist accumulation, except in commercially active areas like Dubai, Bahrain, and Kuwait, where a surplus was produced by a small but stable social group that subsequently acquired economic influence.

Most of the region's inhabitants struggled to eke out a living from the harsh environment. The task of the ruler was confined to passing judgement in disputes arising between individuals. In this he relied on the loyalty of those tribes owing allegiance to him. The degree to which tribal chiefs and the big merchants (if there were any) obeyed him was a measure of the ruler's political authority. When people moved from one place to another, their allegiance to a particular ruler moved with them.

The notion of the state in the modern sense was introduced arbitrarily in order to further British interests: a new system of political rule was imposed on the pre-existing social system, with tribal chiefs now being forced to accept legal responsibility for the members of all tribes that owed them allegiance. This accounts for the chessboard division of the emirates and the various neutral zones between them, and for the difficulty of defining borders even up to the present day. Border disputes sharpened with the initial oil discoveries after the First World War, and were critical in frustrating the cause of unity.

Unbalanced growth began immediately after the First World War. Later, when the pearl trade was hit by the world recession in the thirties, fresh large-scale migrations took place, as people made their way to the new centres of growth. Meanwhile, oil was discovered in Bahrain and commerce took root in Dubai, the latter largely as a result of political developments in Iran, where commercial taxes were raised in the ports opposite Dubai on the Iranian side of the Gulf.

Between 1908 and 1939 the population of Dubai doubled from ten to twenty thousand, while the population of Sharjah dropped from fifteen to five thousand over the same period. Meanwhile, the economies of the other emirates, with the exception of Bahrain and Dubai, suffered crushing blows that reduced them to dire poverty. At one point the ruler of Qatar was even forced to mortgage his private residence.[14] Many of the inhabitants of the coastal region, Qatar, and Kuwait emigrated to Bahrain, where prospects seemed better. This period also saw the emigration of Omani workers, first to Bahrain and later, in the fifties, to Kuwait and eastern Saudi Arabia.

Large-scale migrations continued in the fifties and sixties, particularly from the Omani coast to Kuwait and Qatar. The traditional migrations had made the people of the Gulf culturally homogeneous, and the restrictions imposed by the modern state failed to halt the flow of population from place to place within the region.

The economic and social problems of the Gulf states today are all extremely similar, and require an integrated effort to deal with them. The majority of the population is now made up of foreigners, the exact proportion varying from state to state: immigrants constitute about 55 per cent of the total population, and an even greater proportion of the work-force. Table 2 indicates the break-down of the work-force in the Gulf emirates.

Table 2: Composition of Gulf Work-Force

	1970		1975	
	No.	%	No.	%
Gulf citizens	147,560	31.2	195,115	26.4
Arabs (other than Gulf citizens)	165,934	35.1	231,577	31.3
Asians	83,869	17.8	247,064	33.4
Others	75,295	15.9	66,014	8.9
TOTAL	472,658	100	739,770	100

The table shows that the proportion of the work-force made up by Gulf citizens has decreased, as has the proportion of Arabs, while the number of Asian workers has increased in both absolute and relative terms. The region's Arab identity is increasingly being submerged in an ever-rising tide of multiracialism. Urbanization is also changing the face of the Gulf. By 1975, 93 per cent of the Kuwaiti population were city-dwellers. The figure was 89 per cent for Bahrain, 75 per cent for Qatar, and 62 per cent for the UAE. This degree of urbanization tends to generate city-states, with all their negative social, economic, and security consequences.

The Union of the Nine Emirates

Global, regional, and Arab developments in the second half of the sixties gave rise to uncertainty about the international position of the gulf emirates. The winds of Arab revolution had reached both North and South Yemen. The retreat of colonialism from the region was inevitable, and the enormous wealth now being pumped from beneath the Gulf countries allowed the rulers to expedite their long-term development plans. Britain was suffering from economic pressure and military defeats (Suez, Aden), and in the fifties had become embroiled in a conflict with one of the local powers, Saudi Arabia, over the Buraimi region. At the same time, the United States was looking to establish a major presence in the region, though in a way that suited its ambitions. Washington believed that the regional powers which had emerged as a result of oil production and the spread of education and commerce should play a greater role. In January 1968 Britain announced that it would withdraw from the Gulf region by the end of 1971 and called for the establishment within three years of a union of the nine Gulf emirates: Bahrain, Qatar, and the seven sheikhdoms of the Omani coast.

The British decision to withdraw came as something of a surprise to the local rulers, still mired in their family and tribal conflicts and border disputes. The legacy of conflict made the goal of unity seem unattainable. Yet the beginning of the process came swiftly. On 18 February 1968 Sharjah's *Sawt al-Khalij* (Voice of the Gulf) radio station broadcast a joint proclamation by the rulers of Abu Dhabi (Sheikh Zayid Ibn Sultan Al Nahyan) and Dubai (Sheikh Rashid Ibn Sa'id Al Maktoum) announcing the establishment of a federal union between their two emirates and calling upon the other emirates of the Omani coast, as well as Qatar and Bahrain, to join. The rulers of the other Gulf emirates responded within days, and held a meeting in Dubai on 25–27 February. The result of this meeting was the Dubai Agreement, which became the focal point of political rivalries over the next three years. Despite the rosy picture of future possibilities presented by the agreement, it soon trapped the emirates in a vicious circle.

The Dubai Agreement had three sections. The first sought the establishment of a Union of Arab Emirates; the second dealt with the authorities of the proposed Union; the third contained general protocols. The seventeen articles of the agreement discussed the development of a common foreign and defence policy, and the establishment of a Higher Council to supervise the affairs of the Union and to draw up a full and permanent charter for it. Subsequently, a Council of the Union was to be established to act as its executive body. The Union charter stipulated that the Higher Council would 'take decisions by unanimous agreement'.

One commentator explained the surprisingly swift adoption of the unity project in this way:

If the birth of the baby was simple, its life during the following years was the story of a slow crawl to its ultimate demise. The enthusiasm, good will, and co-operation that masked the first meetings of the rulers of the emirates proved a chance affair never to be repeated. It was a product of the conditions of the time, the extremity of the danger, and the suddenness of Britain's announcement that it intended to withdraw.[15]

A combination of internal and external factors frustrated the development of the Union. Fierce tribal quarrels between the rulers, and each emir's desire to retain as much power as possible in his own particular emirate, plagued the project from the start. Four sessions of the Higher Council were held in 1968 and 1969, the first on 25–26 May 1968 in Abu Dhabi. It broke up over disagreements between the rulers as to how to implement the Dubai Agreement. A second session was scheduled to be held in Abu Dhabi in July. The Abu Dhabi session was indeed held on 6–7 July, but although a number of important decisions were taken, the disagreements had already begun to deepen. One observer commented about the third session, held in Doha:

> Over the five days of continuous meetings, both secret and open, official and unofficial, in night-time sessions, in the council and in committee rooms, the Gulf rulers came to realize that the Union could not be based on the kind of clan loyalties to which they had long been accustomed, that the various historical disputes among them were in fact more serious than they had imagined, and that a modern state could not be constructed on delay, procrastination, and postponement.[16]

The main points of disagreement involved the borders and authority of the government of the Union; the number of seats in the National Council to be given to each of the various emirates; the location of the Union's capital; and the voting procedure in the Higher Council.

By the end of 1969 the pressing circumstances that had caused the rulers to take such prompt action in response to the call for a Union had begun to ease. The Shah's Iran had opposed Bahrain's entry into the Union, and had announced during the July 1968 meeting that Bahrain's presence and its endorsement of the call for Union were provocative acts to which the Iranian government would respond. Tehran's intervention came despite American and British promises that Iran would be given a greater role in the Gulf, particularly since the local powers had agreed to this after the Shah's visit to King Faisal of Saudi Arabia in October 1968.

The recognition of a more prominent Iranian role in the Gulf was formalized in exchange for Iran's renunciation of its claim to Bahrain. In the spring of 1970 a UN commission of inquiry recommended that Bahrain be recognized as an Arab country whose people desire independence. The Security Council then issued a resolution to this effect on 11 May 1970. The people of Bahrain played a positive role in this affair and had high post-independence aspirations. These were given concrete form in the proclamation issued by Sheikh Isa Ibn Salman, the ruler of Bahrain, on 14 August 1971, just before independence. The sheikh justified his decision not to join the Union but to opt for full independence instead, stating:

> Throughout these long discussions, the Bahrain government has consistently emphasized its demand that certain basic principles be respected. Central to these is the drafting of a modern constitution, based on the principle of the separation of powers and the division of responsibilities between the various branches of government, and a guarantee of the rights and freedoms of citizens. None of the above should infringe on the constitutional rights of citizens, as they relate to the principle of their representation in the National Representative Council, which is to be chosen through free and fair elections.[17]

The subsequent experiment with an elected National Representative Council in Bahrain, however, confirmed that the state had simply been attempting to outbid its opponents, and the experiment was abandoned in August 1975. It seems clear that the main reason why Bahrain declined to join the Union was not because it was ultimately convinced of the importance of its own Council. It was, rather, a pretext for reneging on the Dubai Agreement.

Another 'crack' that helped to destroy any potential accord between the parties to the Dubai Agreement was the *coup d'état* in Oman in July 1970, which brought Sultan Qabus to power in place of his bigoted and fanatical father. The coup had been engineered by Britain in an effort to open up Oman and to prevent the revolution against Qabus's father from spreading to the oil-producing countries.

Finally, the Conservative Party in Britain announced that if it were returned to power it would halt or postpone British withdrawal from the Gulf. This eased the tension and uncertainty that had been running high among the various rulers and had spurred the unity experiments.

In September 1970 the death of Nasser removed the central exponent of Arab unity from the political scene. But the most important factor in aborting the Dubai Agreement was the rivalry between the emirs. From the outset the emirates had been split into two camps, one comprising Abu Dhabi and Bahrain, the other Qatar and Dubai. The smaller emirates were divided in their allegiance, with Sharjah attempting to play a mediating role. But the historical disagreements between Qatar and Bahrain—or rather, the sensitivities of the Al Thani and the Al Khalifah—proved impossible to overcome. The Dubai-Qatar camp was based on disagreements between Abu Dhabi and Dubai on the one hand and the existence of family ties on the other (the ruler of Qatar at the time was married to one of the daughters of the ruler of Dubai).

The question of unity came to be seen as a matter of relations between rulers rather than an issue of national sovereignty or of the interests of the majority of the citizens. The Union of the Nine foundered on its attempt to reconcile the traditional privileges enjoyed by the various families (now grown to enormous proportions in the oil era) with the institutions required for the establishment of a modern state.

Qatar was the second signatory of the Dubai Agreement to withdraw from the Union after a covert dispute between Sheikh Ahmad Ibn Ali Al Thani and his then-deputy, Sheikh Khalifah Ibn Ahmad Al Thani, who held that he had a legal right to the throne. This rivalry spilled over into discussions between the Nine, such that Qatar began to put forward proposals considered 'debilitating' to the other members.

The points of disagreement in the plan for the Union of the Nine thus proved greater than the points of agreement, and the loss of interest in it was as dramatic as the initial enthusiasm had been. Its collapse, however, soon led to the emergence of a new plan for a Union of Seven.

The Union of Seven: The United Arab Emirates

The factors that led Bahrain and Qatar to withdraw from the Union of Nine did not result in the withdrawal of any of the other seven emirates (except Ras al-Khaimah, which had hesitated before joining the Union in the first place). But disagreements between the emirates of the Omani coast were nevertheless severe. Border disputes had sharpened as a result of the discovery of oil, and now raged between virtually every emirate and its neighbours. There were border conflicts between Abu Dhabi and Dubai, between Dubai and Sharjah, between Ras al-Khaimah and Oman, and between Abu Dhabi and Saudi Arabia on the one hand and Qatar on the other, not to mention disputes about the continental shelf and the ownership of offshore islands.[18]

There were also long-standing tribal disputes between the ruling families. Objective circumstances nevertheless favoured the establishment of a Union embracing these emirates. Time was a decisive factor, since British withdrawal was scheduled for completion in 1971. It was not until the second half of 1970 that it became apparent that the Union of Nine would fail. The six remaining emirates finally adopted a new constitution for their Union in July 1971, although the decision to prepare such a document had been taken at the first meeting of the Higher Council of the Nine back in May 1968. On 2 December 1971 the new state of the United Arab Emirates was proclaimed in Dubai, with this document as its provisional constitution. The constituent emirates were Abu Dhabi, Dubai, Sharjah, Umm al-Qaiwain, Ajman, and Fujairah; Ras al-Khaimah finally became the seventh member on 10 February 1972. But the Union contained various internal contradictions from its very formation.

As early as the 1950s, Britain had begun urging the seven emirates of the Omani coast to 'co-operate', since Britain now had a real interest in some association of these small units.[19] Oil had been found in the coastal areas and some method of ensuring the region's security and stability and of protecting the drilling projects had to be found. In 1951 Britain set up a unified paramilitary group, the Trucial Oman Levies (later Scouts), made up of Arabs from the interior of Oman and commanded by British officers. The force was supposed to maintain security along the Omani coast. During the same period, and also at the prompting of the British, a Council of the Rulers of the Trucial States was established. This included all seven rulers, and was given power of consultation in matters concerning the coast as a whole. The Council held thirty sessions between 1952 and 1968. In the mid-sixties, oil production in Abu Dhabi reached significant proportions and in 1965, responding to an attempt by certain other Arab countries to provide technical and educational assistance to the emirates of the coast, Britain established the Emirates Development Office, whose task was to study economic and educational development plans. This office was attached to the Council of Rulers.

The Constitution of the Emirates

The provisional constitution of the Union was considered to have come into force on 2 December 1971, the date of the proclamation of the UAE. In theory, this marked a transition from tribal power based on a ruling family to constitutional rule. But the provisions of the constitution soon turned out to have little meaning, since the state was run and decisions were taken much as before.

The constitution stipulates that authority in the UAE is invested in the Higher Council of the Union, which is made up of: the seven rulers; the president and his deputy; the Council of Ministers; the National Council; and the unified judicial system. Article 47 of the constitution states that: 'The Higher Council of the Union is the highest authority in the Union. It is made up of the rulers of all the emirates. Every emirate is to have a single vote.' Article 48 grants the Council far-reaching legislative and executive powers. As for the decisions of the Council, article 49 stipulates: 'The decisions of the Council in matters under debate will be taken by a majority of five of the members, provided that these include the votes of Dubai and Abu Dhabi.'

This article meant that any disputes between Abu Dhabi and Dubai would cause difficulties for the running of the Union, and this, in fact, is what soon happened. Meanwhile, it had been decided that the National Council was to consist of forty members drawn from the various emirates, with Abu Dhabi and Dubai being given eight seats each, Sharjah and Ras al-Khaimah six each, and Ajman, Umm al-Qaiwain and Fujairah four each. It was also stipulated that: 'Each emirate shall be left to decide the manner in which those citizens who are to represent it in the National Council of the Union are chosen' (article 69). (This article had actually been inserted at the time of the plan for the Union of Nine, principally on Bahrain's insistence that its representative to the National Council be chosen directly by the people.)

The provisional constitution stipulated that precedence was to be given to its own rulings and to rulings promulgated by the Union over the laws of the member emirates (article 15), and over legislation, ordinances, and decisions made by the authorities of these emirates.

Article 120 defined those matters over which the Union was to have sole responsibility. They included foreign affairs, defence, the armed forces, security and public order in the permanent capital, Union finances, revenues and taxes, road construction, aerial observation, education, health, currency, nationality and passports, the census and statistics, and the media. Matters in which the Union was to be limited to the passing of legislation (article 121) included labour relations and the work-force, the extradition of criminals, banking, the importing of arms and ammunition not intended for use by the armed forces or security forces of the UAE, and printing and publications. Article 122 stipulated: 'The emirates shall have full responsibility for everything which is not the sole concern of the authorities of the Union in accordance with the conditions of articles 120 and 121.'

Article 123 similarly laid down an exception to the provisions of article 120 concerning the Union's sole responsibility for foreign affairs, stating that it was permissible for the member emirates to conclude limited agreements of a local administrative nature with neighbouring states and nations, provided that these agreements did not conflict with the interests and laws of the Union and that the Higher Council be informed in advance. Emirates were also empowered either to retain their individual membership of OPEC and OAPEC or to withdraw from these organizations. Article 3 of the constitution stipulated: 'The member emirates will exercise sovereignty over their own regional lands and waters in all matters which are not deemed by the constitution to be the area of concern of the Union.'

Some writers, particularly those favourably inclined to the Union, have argued that it has the general characteristics of a centralized state. It has also been claimed that the central state structure is of greater importance than the independent structures of each emirate.[20] Others contend that the provisional constitution was more a treaty than a constitution, since a number of its articles stipulate respect for the sovereignty of the member emirates. Some constitutional experts go further, describing several articles of the provisional constitution as self-contradictory.[21] Whatever legal view of the constitution one may take, the constitutional and political crises of the UAE, and the problems that have arisen with regard to relations between the centre and the individual emirates, would appear to confirm that the agreement that gave rise to the Union was a compromise.

Problems Facing the Union of the Emirates

The problems confronting the states of the UAE today may be classified in two categories: internal and external.

Internal Problems

Internal problems derive mainly from the provisional constitution. Although it stipulates that modifications should be made only to support and strengthen the Union—a constitutional principle that could be instrumental in creating a more powerful Union—repeated attempts to alter the constitution in this sense have all ended in failure, largely because of the simmering dispute between Abu Dhabi and Dubai, which can veto any decision of the Higher Council. The Council itself actually frustrates those people in the emirates who seek unity. Despite the dangers threatening the Gulf, the general weakness of the state structure of the UAE, and the influx of immigrants (which has resulted in a preponderance of foreigners in many of the emirates), rivalries and conflict persist, and the Union has so far been able to preserve only an appearance of cohesion.

Among the outstanding issues of conflict five may be singled out: finance, immigration, defence, the application of Union laws, and general economic policy.

Finance. The provisional constitution states that the Union is to be financed through the levying of taxes by the central authorities. Article 127 stipulates: 'The members of the Union will each set aside a certain proportion of their annual revenue, equal to the amount stipulated by the budgetary law, to cover the costs of the general annual budget.' In the absence of any systematic accounting and with no budget in the modern sense in most of the emirates, the first difficulty that arises is determining the amount of money to be contributed annually by each member. In the beginning, Abu Dhabi, the richest emirate of the Union, undertook to finance the major portion of the budget. Although it had originally been agreed that each emirate should contribute 10 per cent of its income, it was Abu Dhabi that footed the bill in the early years. This was part of an attempt to promote greater centralization. The only other emirate that could have made a significant contribution was Dubai, whose leaders, however, relied on the enthusiasm of Abu Dhabi and paid no money whatsoever. Subsequently, it proved impossible for Abu Dhabi to carry on in this manner.

Four years after the foundation of the UAE, the Higher Council ordered a review of the progress and development of the Union, whose basis was to be strengthened by the drafting of a permanent constitution. Problems had also arisen concerning the unification of the army and foreign immigration, but finance proved to be one of the most intractable issues, and more than one commission was set up to look into the matter. The last of these, the Higher Budget Commission, was set up in 1977 after a financial and constitutional crisis in 1976. This high-level commission was headed by the ruler of Sharjah, Sultan Ibn Muhammad Al Qasimi, and included the ruler of Fujairah, the heir to the throne of Ajman, the minister of finance, and several other ministers. Its task was 'to review all existing laws'. But the commission discontinued its work without giving any reason.[22]

The UAE budget in 1977 totalled 13,150 million dirhams, some 90 per cent of which had been contributed by Abu Dhabi. Dubai's income, meanwhile, was estimated at 3,000–3,500 million dirhams. After Kuwaiti mediation of a second constitutional crisis in early 1979, Dubai agreed to contribute 1,750 million dirhams to the 1979/80 budget. The revenues of the remaining emirates were relatively small, and they were not expected to make substantial contributions, although the sum they were asked to pay is believed to have approached 50 per cent of their incomes.

The intention of the Union authorities in taking this hardline stance was not simply to obtain the financial contributions, they were also hoping to gain tighter control over expenditure and achieve better co-ordination of economic planning. But the relative decline of oil prices is likely to sharpen budget problems, and arguments about the share to be paid by each emirates are certain to rage on.

Immigration. Immigration, housing, nationality and naturalization are burning issues in the UAE. The central problem is that several emirates have shown little or no commitment to the provisions of the constitution, which allocate responsibility for immigration, passports, and nationality to the authorities of the Union. The nationality laws in the UAE—as in the other Gulf states—stipulate that a prospective citizen must have been resident in the country during a particular year or must be a descendant of someone who was then a resident. The law of the Union states that a citizen is: 'Any Arab living in one of the member emirates in the year 1925, or previously, who continued to be normally resident in the country up to the date when this law came into force' (Law on Nationality and Passports, no. 17, 1972, modified by Law no. 10, 1975).[23]

Since the states comprising the UAE experienced large-scale emigration and immigration in the first third of this century, the problems of determining citizenship have proved complex, particularly in commercial centres such as Dubai, which had absorbed many immigrants of non-Arab stock. This is a highly sensitive issue for Abu Dhabi, which restricts the immigration of non-Arabs. Dubai, on the other hand, has adopted a more open-door policy, especially with regard to foreign workers. The question of

immigration thus leads to disputes between those citizens whose
origins are in the Gulf and those who have acquired nationality. The
same conflict also exists in the other Gulf states, though in a less
severe form.

None the less, immigration into the UAE has given rise to steadily
growing popular concern over the past few years. The member
emirates tend to ignore Union decisions on this matter, since the
realities of their economic and commercial situation demand the
entry of foreign workers. At the same time, the Union authorities—
and indeed the general populace—perceive a strategic danger in the
declining relative proportion of citizens, and the fall in the proportion of Arabs. No official statistics on this subject have been
published in recent years,[24] but newspaper reports have referred to
the 'dissolution of the population'.

In 1971, before the establishment of the Union, it was estimated
that about 70 per cent of the population were citizens. By 1979,
following the open-door economic policy, that figure had fallen to 20
per cent according to the most optimistic estimates.[25] Nationalist
writers have made bitter references to this fact. As Muhammad
Ubaid Ghubash, the editor of *Arab Crisis*, wrote:

> Provisionality is an obvious characteristic of life in the UAE.
> The constitution that regulates its life is provisional, as are the
> laws born of this constitution. The capital of the Union is
> provisional. Even the citizen is a provisional citizen who will
> gradually disappear as his place is taken by the permanent
> inhabitants, that flood of immigrants that ceaselessly pours
> into the emirates, destroying the Islamic and Arab character of
> the country and depriving it of its stability and tranquillity.[26]

The nationality and immigration crisis in the UAE has now
reached dangerous proportions. It is, moreover, a complex problem.
The huge industrial and development projects require large numbers of workers. The Jabal Ali industrial project in Dubai, for
instance, needs four hundred thousand workers by the end of 1985,
and the Ruwais industrial region in Abu Dhabi needs one hundred
thousand. Labour, especially non-Arab foreign labour, is desper-
ately needed, but at the same time there is an attempt to apply the
nationality law rigorously to prevent large numbers of residents

from acquiring nationality even if they have lived in the region for the long period prescribed by law. Regulation of the entry of aliens is lax, however. The emirates have an extensive coastline. There are few facilities for guarding the coast, and this makes it easy for people to slip into the country illegally. There are also a number of airports—in Sharjah, Abu Dhabi, and Ras al-Khaimah—each of which is run by the local emirate. The law can easily be applied with varying degrees of rigour by the different airport authorities.

The question of immigration is linked to that of internal and external security. The native inhabitants are frightened of becoming a minority in their own country and are concerned that some change of circumstance could cause them to lose their own land through 'internal invasion'. As one author put it:

> The most important question relating to security . . . is how to solve the population problem. Those in positions of authority seem not to realize the full extent of the danger. When there are four immigrants to every citizen—according to World Bank estimates (Report on the Emirates, 1976/77)—all talk of security becomes a kind of meaningless blather.
>
> There are two internal dangers in the Gulf, with which we must deal while there is still time. The first is the presence of large foreign communities. At present we have friendly relations with the various governments of these people. But governments change, and state policies change with them. It is therefore possible that some foreign government could use its community in our country to hold us to ransom, to impose policies and measures on our land that would be unacceptable to any country claiming to be independent and autonomous. The second danger, from our own compatriots, can be removed by creating conditions that will allow us to cope with grievances of whatever sort—by opening up the channels of democracy and the rule of law.[27]

Defence. One of the issues on which the provisional constitution sought compromise was defence and the armed forces. Article 138 states: 'The Union shall have an army, a navy, and an air force; these are to be trained and officered on a unified basis. The Union will have the power to appoint and dismiss the commander-in-chief and the chief of the General Staff.' Article 142, however, states: 'The member emirates have the right to raise local armed forces. These should be capable of being incorporated into the defence apparatus of the Union if required for defence against any outside aggressor.'

The fact that the various emirates have all retained their own forces shows that they have no real confidence in the centralized power of the Union or in its ability to defend the independence of the small emirates. Unification of the army in the UAE has proved an intractable problem, and negotiations repeatedly came up against a solid wall of indifference during the first four years of the Union. Those favouring unification claimed that it would be impossible to build a powerful independent state as long as the armed forces remained fragmented. But each emirate proceeded to raise its own army. The largest was Abu Dhabi's, which relied on tribes from the interior, other Arabs, and even foreigners; Dubai also undertook to bolster its own defence forces and to supply them with modern military equipment with the help of foreign officers, most of them British. Some of the other emirates copied these two larger ones as best they could. Finally, in May 1975, the Higher Council proposed a solution: the defence forces would be combined into a single Army of the Union that would have the sole right to possess air, land, and sea weapons. The Council also agreed to draft legislation granting the Union authorities the sole right to import arms. A number of committees were set up to study the implementation of this decision. They presented their report to the Higher Council on 6 May 1976. The Council then agreed to unify the land, sea, and air forces of the UAE under a central leadership of the Armed Forces. They also agreed to adopt a single military flag, motto, and uniform.

But disagreements about defence persist, and the lack of co-ordination between military units is a dangerous sign of the fragmented nature of the state, particularly when it is recalled that the UAE army is composed mainly of foreigners. Some reports have estimated that more than twenty-eight different nationalities are represented in the defence forces of the emirates. The majority of these foreigners are Omanis.[28] This is itself a major problem. The size of these armed forces is enormous (the total number of solidiers is equal to about one-third of the whole population), and a memorandum produced by the Council of Ministers and the National Council in March 1979 pointed out that the fragmentation of the armed forces impedes their ability to defend the country.

The Application of Union Laws. Many of the laws passed by the Union have never been applied. The law on printing and publication, for instance, has never been enforced, so that when a number of magazines and newspapers were closed down, it was done in a thoroughly arbitrary fashion. This is typical of many other obstacles the citizens face, including the licensing of cars in various emirates, commercial activities, the drawing up of contracts, and so on.

In early 1979, the most difficult period of the UAE's short history, there were violent popular demonstrations: students, public officials, and others vented mass anger at the lack of official resolve in strengthening the Union. The people demanded the social expression of unity, namely democracy—a question the Council had not even touched on. The 'People's Charter', handed to the head of state in Abu Dhabi by the demonstrators on 29 March 1979, reflected the real demands of the people. The charter stated:

> We will accept no further delay over the question of the internal borders of the emirates; this is an artificial problem. Our forefathers lived and moved about without any conception of borders. Such borders must be abolished for ever.[29]

General Economic Policy. Differences over economic policy constitute the last important difficulty faced by the UAE. Although the state earns its money from oil, there is no unified oil policy. Indeed, the provisional constitution grants each small emirate the right to dispose of its natural wealth independently. Oil has been produced in Abu Dhabi since 1963, in Dubai since 1969, and in small quantities in Sharjah since 1970 and Ras al-Khaimah since 1976. The central state needs a single oil policy. As one commentator has put it:

> The researcher cannot ignore this tendency towards total, or at least relative, independence in this vital sphere. At the same time, the official line is that petroleum activities are subject to central supervision by the Ministry of Oil and Mineral Wealth.[30]

It is crucial for the Union to come to a clear decision on the disposition of natural resources so that the individual emirates do not adopt contradictory policies in this important sector of the economy.

Similarly, some emirates continue to embark on competitive economic projects without regard to the integration of the state. This brings with it the possibility of competition, which would naturally entail the further importation of labour.

External Problems and the Future
The complex internal problems now besetting the UAE might well provide opportunities for any foreign power interested in destroying this entity. The Gulf today is caught up in rapid regional and international changes. It is clear that the internal constitutional and political difficulties of the UAE are in various ways connected with the general regional and global situation.

Even now the state is involved in border disputes with its neighbours. There is an unsettled dispute with Saudi Arabia, even though agreement was supposedly reached in principle in 1974. There are similar problems with Oman, as well as difficulties over maritime borders.

During the seventies, when the small countries of the Gulf emerged into the international arena after their independence from Britain, the Gulf came under the protection of the Shah of Iran. With his overthrow the United States inevitably became directly involved. After the US had threatened to use force to occupy the Gulf oil-producing areas in the event of a crisis, it became important that powerful Arab political units be established in the region. The Iranian revolution has underscored the need for such units. But the emirates' internal fragmentation leaves them vulnerable to interference by any number of foreign powers, and no Arab power is now capable of taking responsibility for the security of this important sector of the larger Arab nation.

During the past few years, rapid social and economic changes have brought a radical transformation in the aspirations of the people of the Arab emirates. Traditional political and tribal structures have held out against these new expectations, and this has led to an unstable internal situation. Many members of the new elite look towards the state president and his entourage to promote the cause of unity and lift the country out of its present political and administrative chaos. But the traditional structures in most of the emirates remain opposed to any genuine and effective integration. As one observer has noted:

> It seems unlikely that the present political structures in the small countries of the Gulf will initiate any serious moves towards an integrated form of union which would allow the emirates to pursue the long-term goal of self-sufficiency. Despite the co-operation between the patriarchal elites, they are wary of one another, since they realize that full co-operation would threaten their power and freedom of operation.[31]

There can be no doubt that the ruling political structure in the smaller emirates depends on tribal and family loyalties. The Union has become a prisoner of the provisional constitution. The first step towards change is therefore to modify various articles of the constitution that impede unity. This, however, can be achieved only through the consent and agreement of the rulers themselves. In the present circumstances, such agreement would appear virtually impossible. The Union has survived because the centre and the individual members have been willing to compromise. But radical changes leading to the emergence of some form of popular democracy are necessary if the new educated forces, who have a genuine interest in strengthening the Union, are to be able to express themselves independently of the traditional political structures. Over the past few years Abu Dhabi's economic clout has been decisive in running the Union. If an economic power rivalling that of Abu Dhabi were to arise, the new social forces might rally round it. The greater the number of sources of economic power, however, the weaker the structure of the Union will become.

Despite all the problems, the progress achieved by the UAE provides some indication of the possibilities for co-operation among Gulf states. Such co-operation dates back to the late seventies, and it is this that we shall examine in the next chapter.

5
Unity:
The First Attempts

In February 1981 the Gulf states announced the formation of the Gulf Co-operation Council (GCC), with its headquarters in Riyadh. Its stated goal was to 'deepen and strengthen the bonds and areas of co-operation between its members in various fields'.[1] The organization has a Higher Council, composed of the heads of state, and a Council of Ministers, which includes the foreign ministers; there is also a Committee for the Resolution of Disputes (which is attached to the Higher Council) and a General Administrative Secretariat. The formation of the GCC marked a new stage of co-operation between the Gulf states, one which differs in both form and content from any previous attempt.

The GCC is significant enough to be discussed separately (see Ch. 6). For the moment, we are concerned with the various forms of collaboration that preceded it. First, however, a terminological point should be clarified. The expression 'Gulf countries' is ambiguous. In the widest sense it can refer to all the states of the region: the six members of the GCC (the UAE, Kuwait, Saudi Arabia, Bahrain, Qatar, Oman) plus Iran and Iraq. In the narrowest sense it means the three emirates of the UAE, Bahrain, and Qatar, together with Oman. More recently, the term has been applied to the *Arab* countries bordering the Gulf: the GCC members plus Iraq. Through most of this chapter, we will be discussing the members of the GCC, which means that we are using the expression 'Gulf countries' in an intermediary sense.

Incentives for Co-operation

The international emergence of the Gulf countries coincided with the sharp rise in oil prices and the increase in demand for oil from the industrialized states. Subsequently the Gulf states came to have real political and economic interests—beyond cultural and ideological incentives—in establishing some formula for co-operation. Virtually all economists are now agreed on the importance of the 'economic integration' of the Gulf countries. These countries are all dependent on a single industry, oil. Most commodities are imported. They have balance of payments surpluses that have led to the deposit or investment of capital abroad. The local markets and local populations are small. They depend on foreign workers. Their capacity to absorb investments is weak, and each individual country has difficulty training administrative and technical cadres.

The recommendations of the economists are based on these and similar observations. Any diversification of sources of income and expansion of capacity will require a regional planning strategy to channel investments, and the use of financial surpluses to establish industries. Moreover, the economists continue, there are two further requirements: first, a single market of relatively large size; and, second, an increase in productive capacity through the use of technology which is, in turn, dependent on the availability of trained personnel. Some writers have also raised other, not specifically economic, arguments. One study, for example, maintains that integration is necessary if equitable regional relations are to be established. Its author holds that the regional redistribution of wealth is not simply a moral necessity, but is also desirable on grounds of security.[2]

Another justification for Gulf co-operation is the general failure of wider Arab co-operation to produce tangible results.[3] Gulf co-operation, however, is not an alternative to Arab co-operation, but an essential element of it. But the economic integration of the Gulf countries may well be a more feasible goal than broader Arab integration, since Gulf infrastructures are still embryonic and no stable superstructures yet exist. The complexities of production, organization, and administration that impede co-operation between some other Arab states are absent here.

On the other hand, the similarities between the economies of the Gulf countries may paradoxically become obstacles to integration, for the longer such integration is deferred, the greater the danger of sharpened rivalry. As one writer has pointed out:

It should be noted that the present development model is creating a set of realities that do not in the least facilitate the process of economic integration—particularly in the Arab oil-producing countries and especially the Gulf countries. For the borders in this region seem less and less temporary or provisional and may not be easily abolished by a process of comprehensive development. The adoption of a single model of development will lead to similar and therefore competing economic structures, thus blocking any trends towards integration, whatever new circumstances may arise.[4]

Forms of Co-operation

Gulf co-operation, which began in the seventies, especially the late seventies, operates on many levels, involving politics, culture, the media, and security. Five principal forms of co-operation may be distinguished: bilateral co-operation; ministerial meetings; joint working parties; joint publicly owned economic institutions; private commercial and commercial-industrial companies. No information whatever is available about military co-operation or the co-ordination of foreign policy. For this reason no analysis of these topics will be attempted in this chapter.

Bilateral Co-operation
The first steps to Gulf co-operation were bilateral. As these countries emerged from colonial rule in the sixties and early seventies, they rapidly sought bilateral agreements. The earliest of these to which we have access is the economic agreement between Kuwait and Iraq, signed in October 1964. After 1972 such agreements proliferated, Kuwait often acting as the principal initiator. Two examples are the economic, educational and media agreement between Kuwait and Bahrain of June 1973, and the economic agreement between Kuwait and the UAE of November 1976 (renewed in December 1978). In June 1973 the UAE and Qatar also signed a series of bilateral agreements guaranteeing the free movement of workers and capital.

These bilateral agreements are primarily concerned with economics and only secondarily with education and sometimes the media. In general they are of limited duration, lasting between three and five years. Some require renegotiation, others are automatically renewable.[5] This kind of agreement, however, was soon superceded by Gulf-wide co-operation in multilateral agreements.

Ministerial Meetings

The first conferences of Gulf ministers were held in the mid-seventies. They have generally led to more specialized multilateral accords and to the establishment of a range of institutions. The first ministerial conference was a gathering of education ministers in October 1975 in Riyadh; the conference was attended by Bahrain, the UAE, Qatar, Kuwait, Saudi Arabia, and Oman.

It was followed by a conference of ministers of information in Abu Dhabi in January 1976, attended by Bahrain, the UAE, Qatar, Kuwait, Saudi Arabia, Oman, and Iraq. A second conference of information ministers was held in Riyadh in October 1977. Subsequent meetings were held in Bahrain (1979), Qatar (1980), and Oman (1981). February 1976 saw the first conference of industry ministers, leading to the establishment of a Gulf organization for industrial investments. Trade and finance ministers met for the first time in Baghdad in October 1977, and subsequently in Riyadh in January 1979. Meanwhile, the first conference of Gulf agricultural ministers was convened in Riyadh in February 1976, to be followed by conferences in Dubai, Qatar, and Kuwait. Social affairs and labour ministers held three conferences, in February 1978, February 1979, and January 1981.

Planning ministers held their first conference in Riyadh in January 1979, their second in Qatar in 1980. Health ministers held their tenth conference in January 1981. In addition to these ministerial conferences, other high-level meetings have been held among central banks and Chambers of Commerce and Industry.

Ministerial conferences have been held in about eight specialist fields. These have given rise to many institutions, companies, and monitoring committees. But the practical actions arising from such conferences sometimes fail to meet the ambitions of the ministers themselves. At the opening ceremony of the tenth conference of Gulf ministers of health in January 1981, the minister from Bahrain remarked:

none the less, allow me to say that in my personal opinion such co-operation has not yet produced sufficient practical results. Nor have results been of the desired standard. Indeed, the difficult historical phase through which the region is now passing demands more profound and far-reaching achievements. Popular Arab sentiment for integration and unity in the Gulf is running ahead of our plans and efforts.[6]

Joint Working Parties

Working parties have been set up on the recommendations of the ministerial conferences in various specialized areas. Their functions are usually consultative.

They include:

The *Gulf Organization for Industrial Investments*, established in February 1976 and with its headquarters in Doha. Its purpose is to co-ordinate industrial co-operation.

The *Joint Institution for the Production of Programmes*, a regional group for the making of television programmes, with its headquarters in Kuwait. Its formation dates from January 1976.

The *Office of the Gulf Ports Union*, established in October 1976.

The *Gulf News Agency*, based in Bahrain. The agency was established in October 1977 as a result of the second conference of ministers of information.

The *Gulf States Arab Education Office*, formed in 1975 and with its headquarters in Riyadh. Its duties include the monitoring of decisions taken by the conferences of ministers of education, and the supervision of joint educational bodies.

The *Arab Centre for Educational Research*, based in Kuwait and attached to the Arab Education Office. Its purpose is to focus research in all areas related to education and to encourage education in the member states. The centre's basic organization dates back to the third conference of education ministers, held in Abu Dhabi in April 1978.

The *Gulf Postal Authority*, which held its first conference in Riyadh in September 1977. Two subsequent conferences were held in 1978 and 1979.

The *Union of Chambers of Commerce and Industry in the Gulf States*, whose basic organization was approved in October 1979 by the second conference of the Chambers of Commerce, Industry, and Agriculture.

The *Conference for the Co-ordination of Television*, which met for the first time in Abu Dhabi in June 1976.

The *Centre for the Documentation of Information in the Gulf*, formally established by the fifth conference of information ministers in February 1980. Its headquarters are in Baghdad.

The *University of the Gulf*. This was first proposed during the fourth conference of education ministers in Bahrain in April 1979. Its foundation was agreed at the fifth conference, in March 1980 in Kuwait. The university is located in Bahrain.

Apart from these institutions there are also many specialist groups, particularly in the field of health, not associated with particular goverment bodies. They include a unified purchasing procedure for many of the medicines available on the world market. A start has also been made towards establishing a local pharmaceutical industry, and it has been agreed to inaugurate a programme of health education to unify medical personnel and establish an innoculation bank for combating malaria.

There have also been innumerable joint study groups on health, education, and the media, and there are other bodies such as the Regional Centre for the Training of Broadcasters, the Regional Centre for Fishing Training, and the Joint Body for Maritime Observation (the agreement under which this was set up also includes Iran, but it has never actually been ratified).

Despite the large number of institutions, there is no comprehensive umbrella organization under which they could all be united. They also suffer from constant changes in the membership of their administrative councils. On the other hand, they have managed to perform some of the services required of them, despite the administrative obstacles. The work done by some of them has been of benefit to the whole Arab world.

Joint Publicly Owned Economic Institutions

Most of the Gulf countries participate in the ministerial meetings and working groups. The economic projects, on the other hand, are less universal. The least wealthy countries are unable to participate consistently in the large-scale economic projects, which include the following:

Gulf Air, which is based in Bahrain and in which all the Gulf countries except Saudi Arabia, Iraq, and Kuwait have a share. Gulf Air was founded in its present form in 1974, after being purchased from the small British company that used to operate air transport in the Gulf.

The *Gulf International Bank*, established in December 1975 and also based in Bahrain. All the Gulf countries except Iraq have shares.

The *Arab Maritime Company*, established in January 1976. Its ships bear the flags of all the Gulf countries except Oman.

The *Joint Company for Maritime Transport*, which was founded in February 1979 and includes only Kuwait, Saudi Arabia, and Qatar.

The *Gulf Petrochemical Industries Company*, based in Bahrain and established in May 1980 as a joint venture of Bahrain, Saudi Arabia, and Kuwait.

It should be noted that there are relatively few official regional economic projects, although there are many bilateral ones.

Private Companies
The establishment of joint or bilateral real estate investment or trading companies represents another aspect of economic co-operation in the Gulf. There are now around thirty such companies (as well as a bank) operating in various sectors. They include, for instance, the Sharjah group, which was the first Gulf bank, the First Gulf Union Company, the Gulf Union Insurance Company, and the Gulf Financial Centre Company.[7]

The status of these companies was hotly debated in the Kuwaiti press, those companies established in the smaller emirates of the UAE causing particular controversy. In the end, many of them were given the right to be listed on the Kuwaiti stock exchange.[8] The companies act as an outlet for Gulf capital, and some have performed useful economic and productive services.

Projects and Agreements Never Implemented

Many Gulf projects and institutions have been discussed but never acted on. Some of these have been the subject of extensive studies and repeated meetings. One example is the project for unifying currencies. Although people are aware that the whole region used a single currency before independence, no practical steps to resolve the issue have as yet been taken.[9]

Another abandoned project is a unified air transport company; numerous meetings have produced no tangible results. The same fate has befallen the Kuwaiti project to establish a railway network between the countries of the region, and the idea of a joint board for the conservation of Gulf animals and plants. Various other agreements have been signed by all parties in the Gulf but never applied. These include an agreement granting the citizens of the various states freedom to pursue commercial and industrial activities and to own real estate throughout the region. Laws dealing with these issues have been promulgated but never properly applied.[10]

Obstacles to Co-operation

Obstacles to co-operation include not only minor administrative and executive problems, but also the lack of clear goals and methods of applying projects. Intentions alone are not enough.

The experiences of other countries highlight one of the preconditions for economic and political co-operation or integration. First, it is necessary for all parties involved to surrender at least a part, if not all, of their local sovereignty. The concept of absolute sovereignty does not accord with the demands of the modern world, and even the most powerful states are now moving towards some forms of economic and political integration.

But the flexible concept of sovereignty is still antithetical to the conceptions held by the Gulf countries. Their traditional, rigid concept of sovereignty is encouraged by a number of external parties who do not wish to see any form of co-operation or integration in the region that might ultimately lead to union.

Gulf co-operation is beset by numerous obstacles, and the problems are ccmplex. Dr Ali Abd al-Rahman al-Khalaf, General Secretary of the Gulf Organization for Industrial Investments, has commented:

> The failure of joint Arab ventures can often be attributed to concomitant political and economic factors. Frequently, however, we ignore one important aspect, namely the role of the planner or organizer of the joint Arab project. Responsibility

for the failure of experimental joint Arab ventures lies first and foremost with those who have done the research into the literature on such ventures, and on the whole question of economic blocs. For such ventures have tended to be established on the basis of unrealistic prospects and irrelevant data. The resulting generalizations have then been hurriedly transformed into political decisions.[11]

Despite all the various problems, Gulf co-operation began in earnest in the late seventies. Such co-operation, therefore, has existed for only a short period compared with similar ventures in other parts of the world. None the less the expectations of the region's inhabitants are as great as the challenges they face. The number of joint institutions is increasing daily, a process that reached a high point at the beginning of the eighties with the establishment of the GCC.

6
The Gulf Co-operation Council

During the late fifties and early sixties the countries which are now members of the GCC were exposed to fundamental internal and external changes. It was a time of upheaval in all Arab states. Arab nationalism was on the rise and manifested itself in the Gulf region in two principal events: the Iraqi revolution of 1958 and the subsequent turmoil there; and the changes in the south-western Arabian peninsula, leading to the war between opposing factions in North Yemen and the ensuing revolution in South Yemen.

These revolutions were a sign of the new forces asserting themselves in the Arab world—forces which would sooner or later leave their mark on the Gulf states. At the end of the Second World War the Gulf societies were living at subsistence level in the shadow of a traditional economy. The inhabitants of these societies earned their living from seafaring or pearl-diving, and had little to contribute to the modern world.

Then, in the space of a few years, the Gulf was plunged into the international arena, and found itself in the midst of a modern economy. The effects of oil wealth began to be felt in the fifties and sixties, just when the progressive forces manifesting themselves in the Arab nationalist movement were awakening. Britain had acted as protector of the Gulf for almost a century and a half, but now found it had to make concessions to these new forces in order to ward off the threat of violence of the kind that had occurred elsewhere. The ground for political independence was being prepared. Kuwait was first, in 1961. Ten years later the smaller countries—Bahrain, Qatar, and the UAE—gained their independence.

Although Saudi Arabia and Oman had never been linked to Britain by any formal protection treaties, it is legitimate to argue that the GCC states attained true political independence only in the sixties and seventies. Moreover, independence was achieved through the traditional elites which had themselves come to power as the result of British policy. As Britain withdrew, power was ceded to those families who were already participating in running the region. The citizens of these countries were not sufficiently politically aware to initiate a revolution or popular uprising against Britain or its allies along the lines of those which broke out in other parts of the Arab world.

Less than ten years separate the advent of political independence in the Gulf states and the outbreak of the Iranian revolution. The 'Nixon doctrine', which called for the promotion of local forces to undertake the defence of Western interests throughout the Third World, seemed at first to succeed in the Gulf. The influence of the Shah rose steadily, and he gave evidence of his determination to play the role of 'policeman of the Gulf' when he occupied two islands in the Straits of Hormuz in 1972. This was followed by his success in 1975 in extracting an agreement from Iraq, settling an old dispute over the Shatt al-Arab region to the advantage of Iran.

It seemed as though Iranian influence was there to stay. Ultimately, however, Iran was plunged into the revolution that led to the overthrow of the Shah and a dramatic change in the system he had helped to build up. The Gulf countries had only recently awakened to the spirit of Arab revolution spreading across from the western part of the Arab world. They now began to hear the reverberations of the slogans of a new revolution deeply rooted in the culture and consciousness of its people. The watchword of the past had been Arab nationalism, but the new slogan was Islam.

Historically, many Iranians—both Shi'is and Sunnis—had emigrated to various Gulf countries. Some of these immigrants were highly successful and had been assimilated into the societies they had entered. But while it proved relatively easy to absorb Iranians of the Sunni faith, many of the Shi'is have tended to retain their own independent culture, customs, and traditions. Like many minority groups, they are politically deprived.

The spirit of political independence was first awakened by the threat posed by the expansion of Arab nationalism (which began to lose some of its initial vigour in the 1960s). But then a new challenge was thrown up, that of fundamentalist Islam, which directly influenced many of the local Shi'i inhabitants and indirectly influenced fundamentalist elements among the Sunni majority.

The political choices on offer to the Gulf states were limited. They could not afford to sit back and observe events, but at the same time they were incapable of seizing the initiative. They had either to call upon some outside power or try to put together some kind of regional force, some regional power base. For various reasons, Iraq was not in a position to play this role. The remaining Gulf states therefore took the one course of action open to them. They set up the GCC, the official purpose of which was to pursue economic and social co-operation.

The Societies of the GCC

The influx of oil money has brought changes in the Gulf states and their societies. New political structures were supposed to fulfil the requirements of the new economic system by spending on education and culture, demographic change, and a transformation of the status of women. But most changes have tended to be fairly super-ficial, linked to the new mode of production and to the brief period within which they were introduced. Two typical indicators in this regard are literacy rates and *per capita* gross national product (GNP).

As regards literacy of citizens over 15 years of age, Kuwait ranks third among the Arab states: 55 per cent of its people can read and write.[1] Only in Lebanon (68 per cent) and Jordan (62 per cent) are the figures higher. Bahrain's literacy rate is 47 per cent while both Saudi Arabia's and Qatar's are about 33 per cent. Oman's is only 20 per cent and in the UAE the figure is no more than 15 per cent.

As regards *per capita* GNP, Kuwait, the UAE, and Qatar head the list: the figures for 1976 are $15,840, $13,990, and $11,400 respectively. They are followed by Saudi Arabia ($6,310), Oman ($4,480), and Bahrain ($2,680). The GCC states thus lead the Arab world.[2] *Per capita* income in some of these countries exceeds even that of the United States. In these terms, these Arab states are the richest countries in the world.

It must be remembered, however, that relatively low proportions of the local populations are economically active. Local workers constitute 22.3 per cent of the total work-force in Saudi Arabia. The percentages for the other GCC members are: Oman 24.9; the UAE

22.3; Bahrain 21.3; Qatar 20.7; Kuwait 19.[3]

There are two reasons for this. First, a high proportion of the local population is under 15 years of age; and second, foreign labour, both Arab and non-Arab, plays an important role in these economies. Foreigners see a chance to earn relatively high wages, while the local population is unable to supply the necessary labour.

Observers are often shocked by the proportion of foreigners in the total population. In Kuwait in 1980, 42 per cent of the inhabitants were foreigners. In the UAE in 1981, the corresponding figure was 63 per cent; in other words, nearly two-thirds of the inhabitants were foreigners.[4] In Saudi Arabia in 1980, non-citizens outnumbered citizens by a ratio of 7 to 3. Figures for Bahrain were 68 per cent citizens, 32 per cent foreigners. Locals constitute only 40 per cent of the population of Qatar. Oman is the exception to the rule: more than 90 per cent of its inhabitants are citizens.

The foreign workers' countries of origin differ in the various Gulf states. In Saudi Arabia and Kuwait most non-local elements come from other Arab countries (the figures are almost 90 per cent and 70 per cent respectively).[5] In the other GCC states Asians make up the majority of the work-force. Most of them come from India and Pakistan, and more recently from Korea and the Philippines. Each day hundreds of these workers arrive at the airports and wait to be transferred to the areas where they are required to work. Some wear T-shirts bearing a map of Saudi Arabia with the legend, 'Go to Saudi Arabia, the land of work opportunity.'

The presence of foreign workers in the Gulf is not a temporary phenomenon: some of them have been working in the region for twenty years or more, and their work is permanent. Filipinos, for example, now work as nurses in hospitals and in clerical posts in local companies. Official sources, however, continue to call them 'temporary workers'.

The GCC countries face two sorts of problem with regard to foreign workers. The first concerns Arabs who have become integrated into Gulf society, share the local culture, and have spent many years working in the region. These people reject all the prejudiced attitudes and discriminatory legislation they encounter from the local citizens. Many of these Arabs would like to be allowed to settle permanently in the Gulf. The Kuwaiti Ministry of the Interior recently established a register for those wishing to become Kuwaiti citizens. Despite the stiff conditions imposed—relating to necessary qualifications and a long period of residence in the country—more than 100,000 Arabs have reportedly applied for citizenship. Most of the applicants are from Syria, Lebanon, Egypt and Sudan. There are also a large number of Palestinians.

The problems faced by non-Arabs are altogether more pressing. These people now constitute the expatriate majority in such countries as the UAE, Qatar, and Bahrain. They have begun to be regarded with extreme suspicion by the local Arab citizens. The legal status of Asian immigrants gives rise to particular concern. A recent report on the treatment of Indian domestic servants comes close to describing their condition as 'servitude':

> Indian domestic servants in Kuwait are the weakest of all the non-Kuwaiti foreign groups subject to discrimination. They are segregated and unable to defend themselves against exploitation. In such a primitive system, moreover, exploitation takes a form comparable to a kind of slavery.[6]

These comments present an extreme view of the problem, but they reveal the extent of awareness of the conditions under which foreign workers live, and hint at the possible consequences if no improvement in their legal and social status is forthcoming. What is required is a balance between the need for foreign workers, and an awareness of the degree to which such workers can be adversely affected because of the threat they are seen to pose to the very existence of these countries. The Gulf states cannot face this challenge individually. Their development plans demand foreign workers, but they fear that the influx of foreigners will finally make them a permanent minority in their own land. Collective action by the GCC states to co-ordinate development plans through the regional distribution of both local and foreign workers is the only real solution.

Policies of the GCC Countries

Saudi Arabia and Oman have undergone few genuine political changes during the past two decades, despite the widely publicized

90

fact that the number of people with doctorates from American universities and now employed in Saudi ministries is greater than the number of people with doctorates in us ministries. Similarly, in Oman Sultan Qabus is surrounded by a circle of highly qualified advisers. Nevertheless real power in Saudi Arabia remains in the hands of the ruling family, and Oman is still controlled by the Sultan himself. Political power is still exercised in the traditional manner and no written constitution has been adopted in either country, despite repeated promises.

The four remaining GCC countries have promulgated modern constitutions. Kuwait was first, in 1962, followed by Bahrain, Qatar, and the UAE in 1972. In Kuwait and Bahrain the constitution provides for elected parliaments with the power to oversee government actions. In Qatar and the UAE, on the other hand, the constitution stipulates a Consultative Council or National Council empowered only to advise the government when the latter so desires.

Critics see these constitutions as no more than slight modifications of the traditional system and hold that power remains in the hands of a hereditary elite: the family of the emirs. Popular participation in the exercise of power seems far off. The degree to which the emirs hold a personal monopoly on power varies from country to country, but in all cases political power is as far removed as possible from the common people.

The GCC states have recently begun to assume a more prominent role in Arab politics. Their oil wealth, combined with Egypt's withdrawal from the confrontation with Israel, have led them to adopt a higher profile in regional politics.

These countries first appeared on the Arab political stage after the 1967 Arab-Israeli war. Nasser's death in 1970 was greeted with some relief by a number of Gulf rulers, whose substantial financial contributions to the Arab cause had not been matched by any real participation in Arab political affairs. At the same time, Britain's 1968 announcement of its intention to withdraw from the Gulf had created a sense of insecurity in the region. It was this that led to the measures designed to unify the Gulf states.

In Kuwait the parliamentary system functioned continuously for some fourteen years, from 1962 to 1976. It was then suspended until 1981, when fresh elections were held in February. The democratic experiment in Bahrain, on the other hand, was short-lived, lasting just three years: parliament was dissolved in August 1975. The consultative councils in Qatar and the UAE were supposed to be temporary, subject to modifications which were to lead, within four years, to a permanent constitution allowing for greater popular participation in power. But the first changes came fully ten years after the establishment of the councils.

Nationalist elements have found it difficult or impossible to bring enough political pressure to bear to force the modernization of the political system. The traditional emirs are quite satisfied with a system that allows them to exercise power in much the same way as they have always done. Saudi Arabia has also encouraged the rulers of the smaller states to resist any move to modernize or liberalize the political system.

In Kuwait and Bahrain the constitution stipulates a democratic system of government and states that ultimate authority lies with the people. In Qatar, the emir also holds the post of prime minister (article 33), while in the UAE the supreme authority is the Higher Council of the Union (see p. 63).

Although the details vary, the basic exercise of power is virtually identical in all countries: the ruling family is in control, in alliance with the merchant class. If it had the will, the local middle class would also have the power to take its place in the chain of authority. Only a small number of citizens, however, belong to the modern working class. In practice, then, the state is able to use its economic power to appease the majority of the local citizens, indeed to incorporate them into the system. The foreign workers, who constitute the majority of the population in many cases, are treated as aliens with no right of access to any economic or political privileges.

The New Reality

The GCC has provided a political framework for genuine co-operation between Gulf states in various fields. The Higher Council —which was to meet twice a year and reach decisions by a unanimous vote—was to formulate general policies in line with the goals set for relations between the Council and other countries. The Council of Ministers was to meet every quarter, its quorum being two-thirds of the member states; it also operated on the principle of unanimity. It was to deal primarily with development but also had to monitor and improve existing joint agreements.

Legal experts believe that there are inconsistencies in the GCC's constitution, particularly with regard to voting procedure in the Higher Council. They have also expressed doubts about the Council's functions. None the less, the organization clearly represents a historic step, the first time these countries have embarked on any co-operative venture without the direction or interference of a foreign power. It remains to be seen, however, what measures the members will actually take to promote the interests of their people. Some regard the Council as a decidedly mixed blessing. While there are those who hold that economic and social benefits will result, and that it may even lead to the introduction of a more modern political system, others regard the organization as nothing more than a political cartel designed to maintain the *status quo* for the benefit of the ruling classes.

Soon after the inauguration of the GCC, two distinct camps emerged. The first was led by Kuwait and enjoyed the open support of the UAE. These two states argued that economic and social co-operation should be at the heart of the project. The other camp, led by Oman, preferred to stress military and security co-operation. Saudi Arabia, Bahrain, and Qatar have tended to act as mediators.

A few weeks before the first Gulf summit, Rashid al-Rashid, Kuwait's deputy foreign minister, affirmed the Kuwaiti position and emphasized his government's opposition to any foreign military presence in the Gulf. The proposed GCC, he said, should seek to liberate the Gulf from all foreign forces, whether American or Soviet. He continued:

> Although the establishment of the new Council represents a step towards Gulf unity, such unity is not in itself the desired goal. To assure the stability of our region, what we need most of all is to pursue efforts to improve the welfare of our people. And this will require a greater degree of general freedom and political participation.[7]

The Omani point of view was put indirectly in a statement issued by the deputy foreign minister, who noted: 'The countries of the Gulf Co-operation Council will be able to defend themselves only if they co-operate with the West.'[8] The semi-official Saudi newspaper *al-Jazirah* also stressed military needs, stating that the West (primarily the US) 'must sell us the weapons we require, but without any interference on the part of its forces'.[9]

Unofficial reaction—and public opinion—was varied. Some representatives of the middle classes welcomed the new move, though not unconditionally, and expressed their hopes for greater economic and political participation and more power-sharing. One leftist organization rejected the entire project, branding it 'an imperialist measure'[10] intended to facilitate the establishment of an American military presence in the region. This was a reference to the repeated public statements of Omani officials. During the period just prior to the June 1981 summit, held in Abu Dhabi, some GCC members seriously considered expelling Oman from the Council. This never happened, however, and the other member states concentrated instead on stressing the Council's economic and social goals.

Another section of Gulf society also detected the hand of reactionary elements in the establishment of the GCC, interpreting it as an attempt to erect yet another bulwark against internal political change. The Council was thus regarded as a means of 'prolonging the life of the current regimes'.

The organization was also rejected by both Iran and Iraq, but for different reasons. Iran's opposition was immediate. Iranian spokesman Ali Khamenei was quoted as saying that the plan was fundamentally anti-Iranian in intent. But no practical measures against the GCC were taken by Iran. Iraq, on the other hand, at first seemed ready to give the GCC its blessing. Subsequently, however, *The Arab Nation*, a newspaper known for its close links with the Iraqi regime, began to raise questions about the Council's goals. Then, in an interview with the Kuwaiti daily *al-Anba* in July 1981, Saddam Hussein, the Iraqi president, indicated his displeasure:

> I have not yet had time to discuss the Co-operation Council with any of my brothers [the heads of state of the GCC countries]. However, I informed my brother Fahd [then heir to the Saudi throne], when he mentioned the matter in my presence in Oman, that he should bear two points in mind: the timing of

the plan, and the manner in which it is announced. I do not consider it appropriate that Iraq, which is fighting Iran on behalf of its brothers, should be excluded from the infant society of the Gulf.

This was a clear indication that Iraq was in fact deliberately excluded from the Council.

Since then official Iraqi reaction has remained negative, although not completely hostile. The semi-official reason for Iraq's exclusion was that there are certain features common to the GCC countries that are not really shared by Iraq. But because of the war with Iran, Iraq needs the co-operation of its Arab neighbours and cannot afford to incur their hostility. Some journalists have suggested that Iraq will ask to join the GCC at some future stage, but it seems unlikely that the other states will agree.

There were also Soviet and American responses to the GCC, albeit cautious. In a nine-point statement issued during a visit to India in December 1980, Brezhnev said that the Soviet Union would respect the neutrality of the Gulf countries if the United States would do likewise.

Washington, meanwhile, spent much time discussing the plans for a Rapid Deployment Force and the joint manoeuvres with Egyptian forces. The United States also made it clear that it wanted land bases in the Gulf. This, of course, would challenge the neutrality of the region, and some believe that the GCC is extraordinarily well suited to US desires to create a new local power base.

Future Challenges

The eighties will throw up new challenges for the Gulf states, both internally and externally. Demands for political and economic participation and a more equitable distribution of wealth will encourage the modernization of the political process. Bedouin tribalism and the 'bedouinocracy' will confront demands for a share of power by the growing middle class. This may lead to some form of internal conflict.

The government face a sharp alternative: either they must

persuade their citizens to work, which would require touch policies that might provoke violent political reactions, or they must go on importing foreign labour, and accept the dangerous consequences.

Externally, the present regimes face mounting pressure from superpower rivalries, denounced locally as 'imperialism' and 'communism'. The Iranian revolution and the Islamic 'vanguard' also represent a serious challenge. Many young people, Sunnis and Shi'is alike, are sympathetic to Islamic revivalism, a consequence of the fact that swift economic growth has been accompanied by extremely limited political development.

The GCC initially grappled with a number of key strategic issues. Had these been solved, the result might have been radical changes in economic and political structures of great benefit to Gulf Arabs. But strategic questions have gradually faded from the agenda, and their place has been taken by short-term tactical matters of economic and cultural co-ordination. The new machinery has thus failed to achieve practical results, sinking instead into bureaucratic diversions.

On the other hand, it must be acknowledged that many of these tactical issues have been quietly dealt with. The economic treaty, for instance, will provide genuine benefits for the people in the future. Similarly, the new institutions and plans will have positive results, the importance of which should not be underestimated.

In the final analysis, however, the GCC's plans will continue to be frustrated and thwarted until proper emphasis is laid on the principles of the charter, and practical steps on strategic issues are taken.

7
Culture and Cultural Development

The Gulf has been described as a cultural meeting-point. Its inhabitants are part of an Arab and Islamic entity; they belong to a deeply rooted Arab-Islamic culture. But the region borders on both Islamic but non-Arab, and non-Islamic, cultures, and its people have been influenced to varying degrees by Iranian and Indian cultures.

Historically, the people of the Gulf lived on the meagre economic surpluses produced in the pearl-diving seasons and through minor agriculture and trade. When surpluses were relatively high, the inhabitants—in particular, the sedentary people of the large villages —found sufficient time to produce a distinctive culture which combined the Arab legacy with elements taken from the cultures of Persia, India, and Africa.

Buildings in the region, for example, are constructed in the same way as those of the Persian and Indian coasts, and the artefacts of everyday life, such as beds and wardrobes, combine local raw materials with techniques introduced by immigrants and traders from neighbouring lands.

Intellectual production was always closely linked to material production. Songs connected with diving, travel, military parades, agriculture, and construction work were common. In pre-oil days, the *nahham*, or chanter aboard ship, encouraging the divers with his powerful voice, was not simply a singer. He was usually a diver or hoister himself.

The traditional culture essentially revolved around material production. It was based on a general heritage that included religious instruction and the production of poetry in both classical and vernacular Arabic (the latter was called *nabat* poetry). Poetry was a link between the present and the past—and it is poetry that has been in the forefront of the modern cultural revival of the Gulf.

Most poets moved back and forth between whichever Gulf societies possessed an economic surplus. It is possible, of course, to link any particular poet to one or other of the modern political entities. But a more realistic attitude is to consider them Gulf society poets.

A figure like Abd al-Jalil al-Tabataba'i, for instance, exercised an influence not only in Basra, but also in Kuwait, Bahrain, and Qatar. The same is true of Muhammad Ibn Mani (originally from Najd, in the Arabian interior), Abd al-Aziz al-Rashid (Kuwait and Bahrain), Qasim al-Mu'awida (Bahrain and Qatar), Isa al-Qatami Bihar, a Kuwaiti who worked as a judge in Oman, Muhammad Ibn Athimain (Najd and the Gulf), Khalid al-Faraj (Bahrain and Kuwait), Abdallah Bilkhair (who may have come from Hadhramawt, or perhaps Hijaz), and many others. Nor can the modern generation of literary figures, intellectuals, and administrative leaders be precisely associated with one or another state. Immigrants (and their descendants) from the coastal regions of Iran, many of whom were Sunni Muslims like the inhabitants of the Gulf countries, were swiftly assimilated, and some have played major roles in religious instruction and culture. They have also had a reforming influence on their fellows in the region.

Traditional forms of education like the Koranic schools gradually gave way, in the early twentieth century, to the beginnings of modern education. The Mubarakiya school was established in Kuwait in 1912, the Khalifiya school in Bahrain in 1919, and the Dubai school in the same year. This was followed by limited activities in publishing, such as the launch of *Kuwait* magazine by Abd al-Aziz al-Rashid in 1928, and the *Bahrain* newspaper by Abdallah al-Zayid in 1939. The new intellectual ferment found a relatively favourable environment in the new schools, where education was to some extent organized on modern lines. Publications like *Kuwait* and *Bahrain* helped to spread the influence of new reforming trends that had begun to take hold in the Arab world, especially in Egypt and Greater Syria. In Kuwait and Bahrain cultural clubs sprang up where young people would meet to discuss articles published in the Arab press and to follow the development of the anti-imperialist struggle in the other Arab states. These clubs, newspapers, and other publications pioneered the introduction into the small Gulf societies of new cultural elements drawn from Arab and Islamic history. Such activities were facilitated by the economic surplus, which now allowed certain social groups, particularly merchants, to provide their sons with an education abroad (notably in India, where some of the beneficiaries of this education went on to take up posts in the British administration).

These enlightened individuals of the reformist trend met strong opposition from ignorant traditionalists and the colonial authorities, who felt that such 'ideas' would ultimately prove detrimental to their own position.[1] The infant clubs and cultural magazines were soon strangled by restrictions, and education fell under the control of those who sought to prevent its expansion. None the less, the progress of this initial period provided the basis for subsequent development. A first generation had sown new seeds in these societies.

In the period following the Second World War, the Gulf emerged from the extreme isolation that had been imposed by colonialism, particularly in the early twentieth century. Although this isolation had distorted the Arab character of the Gulf, the attachment of the local Arab population to their land enabled the region to preserve its Arab and Islamic identity and to embark on a process of self-discovery. Such a project cannot be considered complete as long as any divisions remain, nor can it advance under any form of absolute rule.

The fifties saw a revival of the cultural clubs and also of literary magazines, which now resumed publication, especially *al-Ba'tha* (the Mission) in Kuwait, and *Sawt al-Bahrain* (The Voice of Bahrain). The former was published in Cairo between 1939 and 1954 by the Kuwaiti education mission. Until 1950 it was run by Abd al-Aziz Hussein, and thereafter by Abdallah Zakari al-Ansari. *Al-Ba'tha* promoted the cause of modernism through articles contributed by Kuwaiti and other Gulf writers. One curious fact is that the magazine used to publish a guide to 'Programmes on Radio Kuwait' as a token of its desire for such a station: in fact, no such radio station existed. Under al-Ansari there was a special issue of *al-Ba'tha* devoted to Bahrain. This same period saw writings by women authors from the Gulf dealing openly with political, social, family, and women's affairs. Some women used their own names, others wrote under pseudonyms.

There was also a literary and political debate organized by the

National Cultural Club in Kuwait on the question, 'Is a just despotism preferable to democracy?' Arab writers such as Awni Farsakh and Abd al-Razzaq al-Basir participated in this debate, which was broadcast in its entirety by *Sawt al-Bahrain*. Additional contributions by writers and readers were broadcast in subsequent editions of the programme. The response among intellectuals was impressive: Hussein Darwish and Abdallah al-Ta'i from Oman, and Salih Shihab from Kuwait participated, as did others from the east of the Arabian peninsula. *Swat al-Bahrain* was the organ of progressive-minded opinion in the Gulf during this period.

The Shape of Gulf Society

One of the most striking features of the Gulf countries has been the rapid increase in population. During the past thirty years some countries have seen the number of their inhabitants triple. Projections suggest that the demographic expansion will continue.

Table 3: Estimated Population of the Gulf Countries

	1980	1990	2000
Saudi Arabia	8,367,000	11,458,000	15,565,000
Kuwait	1,372,000	2,194,000	3,166,000
Oman	891,000	1,218,000	1,615,000
UAE	796,000	1,215,000	1,635,000
Bahrain	302,000	416,000	538,000
Qatar	200,000	326,000	434,000
TOTAL	11,928,000	16,827,000	22,953,000

The projections indicate that the present population of the region (about 12 million) will have risen to some 23 million by the year 2000.

This important demographic change should be viewed with other indicators that provide information about the local cultural balance, including the proportion of foreigners of non-Arab or non-Islamic origin (apart from differences that may exist within these groups).

Another significant indicator is the high proportion of young people. Statistics suggest that by the year 2000 people aged between 6 and 23 will make up 42.8 per cent of the population. These figures predict a society of young people—a fact that calls for a sense of cultural responsibility. This society will be concentrated in large urban centres. Finally, the rapidly rising life expectancy should be noted. In Saudi Arabia, for example, average life expectancy in 1978 was 53, compared with 38 just fifteen years previously. In Kuwait it was 69 in 1978, compared with 60 only eighteen years earlier.[2]

These social indicators, the products of economic growth since the Second World War, show that Gulf society is favourably poised for cultural development. Education, the economic abundance created by oil revenues, the increasing amount of time devoted to recreation, the spread of means of communication like radio and television, and the consequent emergence of a new life-style have all played a part in liberating Gulf Arabs, especially the young, from many of the economic woes that previously afflicted them.

To what extent has the new life-style produced a culture which is capable of choice? It is generally agreed that there is a close connection between culture, education, and mass communication. Although the last two are an inseparable part of culture in the wider sense, they both require separate examination.

Education

Since the fifties the Gulf countries have undergone a virtual revolution in education in both quantitative and (less strikingly) qualitative terms.

Education began expanding in the fifties and sixties, but the seventies was the time of greatest progress. In 1970 only 42.1 per cent of children aged 6–11 were registered in primary schools in the six states of the GCC plus Iraq; by 1980 the figure had increased to 66.9 per cent. This represents an absolute increase of 1,648,000 children at primary school. The spread of secondary education was also striking: 28.7 per cent of youth aged between 12 and 17 were at secondary school in 1970, and 48.7 per cent in 1980. Over the same period, the percentage of 18- to 23-year-olds registered in higher education rose from 7.8 to 18.5. There is every reason to believe that these figures will continue to rise.

There are now nine universities in the GCC countries, six of them in Saudi Arabia. Two more are planned, one in Bahrain and the other in Oman. In all, there are now four business and economics faculties, six faculties of secular and Islamic law, fifteen of Arabic language and arts, eleven of education, nine of science, eight of engineering and oil, eight of medical science, three of agriculture and veterinary medicine, and seven of Islamic studies. In both university and pre-university education, there is a concentration on arts, social sciences, and religion, while other fields are under-represented. There are no university faculties specializing in the fine arts, physical education, or music.

In the Gulf, as in the rest of the Arab world, education has been the subject of heated debate. Gulf education has generally taken its cue from Egypt, where a protracted debate still rages about how to reconcile demands that the education system should transmit traditional knowledge with the fact that the system itself has been taken over from the West. How can a balance be achieved between tradition and imitation, inertia and renewal?

The crux of the problem is this: how can education present areas of knowledge, science, and technology to the people of a society without adversely affecting their beliefs and values? In the late thirties Taha Hussein, the great Egyptian writer and educationalist, made this comment about the role of education and the cultural future of the Arabs:

> It is an incontestable fact that since the last century all our educational establishments, courses, and curricula have been entirely constructed on the European model; in our primary, secondary, and tertiary education we have been forming our children in a thoroughly European mould. . . . It would be ridiculous for us to refuse to accept the technical aspects of Western civilization. Indeed, the radio has reached even into al-Azhar mosque and university, and the rector himself has used it to address Muslims all over the world. . . . Whatever the superficial differences, our mental life is basically European, our system of government comes from Europe—even the system of absolute rule came to us from Europe. In our administrative and legislative systems, and even in our

education system, we are using European models.

Taha Hussein was followed by others who criticized the entire Egyptian education system. Referring to those Egyptians brought up under the vacuous education system introduced by Dunlop as 'the Dunlop generation', Muhammad Mahmoud Shakir wrote: 'Dunlop arrived on 17 March 1897 and established a destructive system of education in this country which unfortunately has continued right up to the present.'[3] Shakir's complaint was that the Dunlop generation failed to combine elements of their own culture with those of modern education. This point has been taken up by many others, including Taha Hussein:

> Scholarly institutions are not simply schools. They are, fundamentally, cultural environments in the widest sense of the word. This is why I say that the university is an environment in which not only the world but also the cultured civilized personality is shaped. . . . If a university fails to achieve this goal, it is no more than a humble school.

It should be added that Dunlop alone is not to blame: the succeeding generations also did education in the Arab world a disservice through their own shortcomings.

The basic fact remains that we are in need of an intellectual and industrial revolution of the sort that took place, and indeed is still taking place, in the West—with all the innovation and creativity in political thinking that this implies: an intellectual revolution that has brought about an increase in the capacity and discipline of human thought and has provided various methods, procedures, and tools of inquiry and research for the human race. But how can this be reconciled with the perceived reality of dependency and underdevelopment? In other words, how can we come to terms with science and technology without compromising our values and beliefs?

There are several schools of thought regarding the problem of general and higher education in the Gulf. Some criticize the system as a system, while others object to the pressure to link education to values. Some denounce the division of education into arts and sciences; yet others see the central difficulty as being the tendency to emphasize things that are really the concern of other domains, while ignoring other questions of vital concern.

I would argue that there are three principal interconnected factors. The first concerns the relationship between inherited wisdom and the laws of rationality, between traditional and creative culture. One Islamic thinker, Malik Ibn Nabi, summed up the matter by comparing the attitudes of the Arab world and Japan to Western civilization:

> The Japanese have taken up the attitude of a student towards Western civilization, whereas we have adopted that of a customer. We have imported certain intellectual aspects of Western civilization, but separately from the material objects that civilization produces.[4]

The second factor is related to the assimilation of knowledge and technology. Here it is important to understand that science is neither the enemy nor the ally of religion. Science is neutral in this respect, in that it strives to provide an explanation for the development of life through causal laws, while religion deals with transcendental questions. Science belongs to the sphere of knowledge that can be experienced by the senses, while religion belongs to the sphere of faith. The problem arises if an extreme position is adopted in which science is held to be opposed to religion, or religion to science. Vast numbers of people in the Arab world adopt one position or the other.

The third factor is the democratic dimension of education: the participation of the mass of the people in planning and implementing education policies.

These three factors—the balance between knowledge and values, the reconciling of science and religion, and the democratization of education—provide the principal keys for building a modern education system that can assimilate science and technology and place them at the service of society.

In the Gulf, as elsewhere in the world today, an open cultural rivalry has emerged between education systems and the media. Television, now a global medium, has become a prime channel for disseminating culture and promoting cultural change. Two basic factors have helped to enhance the influence of television in the Gulf countries: the low literacy rate and the new life-style made possible by oil money, in which watching television is regarded as a basic leisure activity.

Gulf television stations began in the sixties and expanded throughout the seventies and eighties. Because of operating conditions, viewers in a number of countries are able to watch the television services of neighbouring states, which has widened viewing circles beyond the restrictions imposed by the political boundaries of a single country.

A preliminary survey of programming in the GCC countries (excluding Saudi Arabia and Oman) indicated that in 1979 the percentage break-down of programmes was: cultural programmes 16.68; variety 13.76; sport 20.49; films 12.03; family and children's programmes 11.82; religious 6.92; other 18.3.[5]

The biggest exporter of television programmes to the Gulf is the United States, while Egypt is the biggest Arab exporter. Gulf television companies work through agents who handle the importing of all types of programmes. Though few in number, these agents hold a virtual monopoly and are able to impose specific tastes on the viewing public. Despite the many attempts to control programmes, television in the Gulf contributes, both directly and indirectly, to promoting a consumer culture.

The cultural invasion via television is not confined to the Gulf region. A study published in the seventies indicated that between one and two hundred thousand hours of television were sold annually by American companies world-wide. Approximately a third of the total went to Latin America, another third to the Far East and Middle East, and the rest to Western Europe. American production companies are often prepared to sell programmes to foreign countries at well below production cost, because they will normally have made their profits from the initial sale on the US market.

It is well known that educated people in the Third World consume more American (and in general, Western) programmes than do uneducated, largely rural people. There is thus a direct link between Western education and the Western media, now controlled by an enormous industry owned by multinational companies. A dominant cultural model is being promoted throughout the world today. One possible response is to use the potential power of the mass media to reinforce indigenous culture rather than alienate it.

Cultural Trends Today

Cultural and intellectual life in the Gulf today is a strange mixture. The same factors that have increased access to culture are simultaneously retarding it. Rising expectations have led to greater problems, and the dominant spirit of consumerism is inducing a form of cultural superficiality.

Before the discovery of oil, the art, dance, thought, and literature of the Gulf were linked directly to everyday life, for there were no specialists of artistic creation. There was a kind of 'cultural public library'; the producer of culture lived within and gave expression to the environment, reflecting material and spiritual deprivation, but also the desire for a better life.

With development, cultural alienation has become confused with genuine culture. Meaningless songs and dreadful serials were of a piece with the phenomenon of the petro-doctorate. The seeds of creative culture were covered by the dust of affectation, and the genuine was confused with the utterly worthless. Cultural alienation has mounted steadily.

One of the signs of this alienation is the tension between primitive religious views and the need to come to terms with science and secularism—it is a tension between traditional values, and the values of the contemporary world forced upon people through the media, and which they absorb through trips to foreign countries. This has led to a 'split personality' among the people of the Gulf.

A preference for the facile and uncomplicated, an aversion to abstraction and intellectual effort, and the precedence accorded material over spiritual values are among the most obvious features of the cultural rupture in Gulf society today.

Two principal cultural trends may be distinguished. One inclines towards liberal thought, is humanistically orientated, and avails itself of scientific methodology in analysing social problems. Moralists, radicals, and enlightened religious thinkers are all found within this trend. The other current may be described as religious extremism. Its adherents' thinking is ossified, excessively concerned with literalism, and orientated towards questions of behaviour rather than belief. Such people are obsessed with details relating to matters like contact between the sexes, female clothing, men's beards, and whether images are permitted or forbidden in Islam. The greater these people's concern for the literal meaning of the various religious texts, the less they are able to keep up with the modern world and the narrower is the area to which these texts are applicable.

Cultural life in the Gulf today is thus in the grip of the conflicting currents now traversing the entire Arab world, although the general influence of culture in fact remains fairly weak. The passivity with which the citizens greet events is simply a reflection of widespread cultural alienation.

Serious attempts are now being made within this society to combat the arbitrary use of censorship by the bureaucracy, to halt the decline into a culture based on illusion, and to resist the rapid rise of a uniform cultural model born of the global culture industry. But independence and unity can be achieved only through a democratic culture; this is how the people of the Gulf will be able to express themselves, to engage in the process of self-discovery, and to restore their own identities. It is an integral project that must be carried out within the framework of a humanistic Arab and Islamic culture.

8
Women

Has oil altered the position of women in the Gulf? The answer is both yes and no. A more productive formulation of the question would be: what influences, both positive and negative, have come into play since the discovery of oil, and how have these affected the position of women in Gulf society?

Many authors treat the question of Arab and Gulf women from a narrow viewpoint, as if women were analogous to a minority group subject to majority pressure. A stereotype of Gulf women has emerged, according to which they are obsessed with 'luxury'. One author states, for example:

> Extravagance . . . has become a distinguishing feature of many Kuwaiti women. The trappings of luxury with which such women now surround themselves consume a great deal of both time and money, to an extent unknown in most countries of the developed world.[1]

But no attempt is made to relate such an observation to the more general realities of society as a whole, from which it cannot reasonably be separated. The position of women is an integral part of society itself, and must be treated as such.

Three Key Issues

The issue of women in Gulf society is but one element in the whole problem of development. Social underdevelopment is among the most evident features of Arab society and manifests itself in all aspects of life, whether economic, social, or cultural. The problem of the position of women therefore goes deeper than the question of whether they enjoy formal legal equality, the right to education and work, or to accompany men on outings or to clubs. I would argue that the problem faced by women in the Gulf, and in the Arab world in general, is that of their awareness of their own humanity and of society's awareness that women are human beings. The people of the Arab world must be liberated from fear and want; their material and spiritual capacities must be released so that they enjoy social, economic, and political freedom within the context of general social welfare. Awareness of women's humanity (on the part of men and women alike) is therefore a vital first step.

A second general issue that must be raised at the outset is the value attached to the education and labour of Gulf women. Many studies have attributed great importance to the degree of female participation in the labour-market and to the rising number of women involved in academic study. The studies published so far show that there are fewer educated or working women (apart from those engaged in handicrafts and agricultural labour) in the Arab world than in other cultural environments.[2] But we must ask ourselves what such bald statistics really mean.

I would not wish to belittle the importance of figures on the employment of women or their involvement in education. There is no doubt that in many societies these two factors provide women with a number of basic advantages. But excessive reliance on figures is apt to be misleading, especially in Third World countries, and most especially in the Gulf countries. The mere fact that women are working or go to school may not tell us very much about the extent to which they are accepted as citizens and as human beings. For instance, women are often restricted to specific jobs like teaching or the social services, and although they are permitted to learn to read and write, they are not allowed to overcome the wider problems of cultural illiteracy. In some Gulf societies there are now relatively large numbers of women in employment. But many of them find (and this holds true for men as well) that there is not actually any work for them to do. As one author put it: 'It is common knowledge that the civil servant in Kuwait doesn't have any work to do.'[3] Such comments may seem imprecise, but they offer some insight into a fundamental issue: production and productivity in the Arab oil societies today.

Figures on education must likewise be read with caution, for education is often unable to demolish other obstacles. One study concludes:

> Research has shown that the achievement of good academic results and a high standard in English at the secondary school level (both conditions for admission to the Faculty of Medicine in Jeddah) are not necessarily among the factors determining whether Saudi girls decide to pursue the study of medicine. Similarly, poor English does not constitute an obstacle to study. Twenty-one per cent of the girls who abandon the study of medicine did so because they got married, 50 per cent because they decided they did not want to study medicine after all, and 29 per cent withdrew for unknown reasons . . . the latter possibly including the lack of a guardian to escort them to the faculty, an inability to get used to the university atmosphere or to living in student accommodation on campus, and apprehension that the studies they would subsequently have to undertake in hospitals might place them in a pre-dominantly male environment.[4]

Since education reflects the dominant socio-economic system, there is no real hope that the prevailing education systems will help bring about any real qualitative improvement in the position of women. Education (for men and women alike) continues to be devoid of any real content or of any clear perspective on development.

Finally, we must consider the general consciousness of Arab women. Consciousness always reflects the natural and social environment. The limited consciousness of Gulf Arab women today is further restricted by political and economic realities and by the influence of the ruling social groups, which are linked to the West, and whose interests coincide with that false consciousness. It has often been pointed out, for example, that Gulf Arab women do not participate in political life, that they are regarded as weak, emotional beings in need of the guidance and supervision of others, that their ambitions are confined to working in certain specific sectors (like government employment), and that they are supposed to avoid the company of men during education and at work.

Such ideas are widely absorbed by women in the Arab Gulf societies through official education, radio and television. This gives rise to a false consciousness. It is, of course, unrealistic to expect the media to seek to provide a comprehensive, valid alternative. In an article written several years ago, I argued:

> This issue of the position of women in the Gulf must not be seen as one which concerns women alone. The solution to this problem lies in women achieving equality with men. In my view, the basic task is to do away with exploitation in Gulf society in all its forms.

The point remains valid today.

Continuity and Change

Gulf society is profoundly contradictory. It contains elements of both desert and urban life, and despite rapid economic expansion, it remains dominated by tribal relations. The ensuing contradictions are apparent both in the family and in the social position of women. Traditionally, the societies of the Gulf enjoyed only small economic surpluses, and what division of labour existed was a division between men and women. These societies were not 'primitive' in the anthropological sense. They were quite stable, and their cultural and religious heritage had a profound influence on social relations.

The decisive social factor was the phenomenon of tribal alliances, both within single tribes and between groups of tribes linked by real or supposed blood relations or relations of allegiance and dependence. As these societies came under the influence of modern colonialism, and especially after the discovery of oil, they were increasingly incorporated into the Western capitalist market. This transformation had an adverse effect, initially through the contact with colonialism and subsequently through the economic changes brought about by oil and the damage wrought to the existing economic and social structure. Most previous economic activities were destroyed, and the Gulf became dependent on a 'modern economy'.

Colonialism and imperialism encouraged the maintenance of the system of tribal kinship links, since it enabled the foreign power to deal with an internal authority with the backing of the traditional social structure. The policy of 'divide and rule' suited both colonialists and tribal leaders. The most powerful clan, which owed its dominance to the possession of the biggest economic surplus, became the ruling tribe, and won the allegiance of the mercantile and martial tribal groupings. The colonial power also fostered disagreements between the tribes; these usually concerned land and water, and, more recently, commercial advantage and political power.

The family and the tribe thus became the pillars of the new states. The number of sons and wives a man possessed remained an index of social worth. There were no real changes of content in the relationship of marriage or in the relations between women and the broader family.

Even today, family and kinship relations are strengthened through marriage, which is therefore not a personal matter between a man and a woman motivated by personal attachment, but a social relationship in which certain kinds of behaviour are permitted and others forbidden. The rules are enforced so rigidly that if they are broken a husband and wife may be separated or one of the partners killed. Neither education nor the new economic situation has done much to change this state of affairs. Marriage between an *asil* and a *baisari* is still forbidden by both society and the family.[5] The economic and political rationale for such a prohibition is to keep wealth and power in the hands of those who already possess them.

Marriage is thus a social matter, and the sheikh or tribal ruler can have as many wives as he wants. This enables him to have more sons (a symbol of his authority and power) and creates bonds of allegiance with other tribes and families, thus maintaining stable authority. There are no restrictions on intermarriage between *asil* families (which are all considered to be related by blood), but it is generally (though no longer universally) forbidden for members of a particular clan to marry outside the family, even if there are commercial and political ties between the families concerned.

One might expect that the incorporation of the Gulf societies into the Western capitalist market would have led to the emergence of new, class-based divisions of labour. But the form of economic incorporation that occurred permitted the development of no more than primitive expressions of the working, middle, and upper classes. Both bonds and disagreements between the traditional groups (tribal and religious) were encouraged, and this retarded the growth of distinctive new class formations. The widespread phenomenon of marriage between cousins (on the father's side) has preserved traditional family and kinship relations; indeed the maintenance of family property and the family and tribal groupings is still a prerequisite for social acceptability.

Although the form of property ownership in traditional Gulf society was simpler than it is now, in practice women were not able to own property independently of their husbands. Theoretically they could own and inherit property, but such theoretical rights, even today, are accorded only in very restricted areas. The husband still remains the direct or indirect guardian of his wife's property, a situation bolstered by the fact that women's social and cultural isolation tends to make them incapable of exercising even those rights to which they are legally entitled.

Generally speaking, women are still considered the private property of men. Gulf societies have traditionally viewed women as the bearer of family honour—this is still true today. Although older forms of seclusion have changed because of modern economic conditions, the content has remained the same. Traditionally, when a girl in Gulf society reached the age of 'maturity' (roughly between 9 and 12 years old), she would wear the chador or the *burqa* (face veil) and remain in her parents' house until she was married off. Even though such 'protection' is no longer as prevalent as it once was, at least among the educated classes, the real (especially psychological) content has changed little. Gulf men still believe that any socially undesirable behaviour on the part of the women sullies the honour of the family. Following a period of relative freedom in educated Gulf society in the sixties, 'neo-traditionalists' began to make their weight felt, and many women started wearing the *hijab*, or veil, again.[6] Some people believe that what such neo-traditionalists are actually advocating is not merely a superficial form of 'protection', but a return to the practice of previous generations: the total seclusion of women.

The current debate about the veiling of women reveals the social impact of the issue. On the one hand, the abandonment of Western women's garb (and the consequent reduction of spending on clothes) is one of the positive manifestations of this society's struggle against its present state of dependence. Yet the manner in which the neo-traditionalists approach the issue implies a whole series of behaviour patterns—for example, women's seclusion from men while studying and at work, the acceptance of polygamy and of a secondary role for women in the home, and even a refusal to allow women into areas of education that might subsequently lead them to associate with men.

The dispute between neo-traditionalists and modernists about the position of women also has a cultural dimension, reflecting disagreement between the two groups about the interpretation of the national heritage with regard to many other questions too. The question of women has become a focal point because the neo-traditionalists feel that there are certain 'values', customs, and traditions to which most people still adhere—or at least dare not challenge openly.

During the sixties and early seventies, Gulf society, in conditions of national struggle, took a positive view of the liberation of women, welcoming their emergence from isolation and their entry into education. The symbol of their isolation, namely the veil in its various traditional forms, was starting to be abandoned, especially by young women. Back in the mid-fifties women in Kuwait and Bahrain had begun to participate in politics together with men, and some young women burned their veils and chadors in protest against obstacles to their full participation in social affairs. A decade or so later, these pioneer women faced opposition from younger women of the new generation because of the mini-skirt—which was felt to be taking things to excess and abusing women's freedom. By the mid-seventies they once again had to endure the wrath of the neo-traditionalists, and of some young women of this third generation, who now support the call for the reimposition of the veil. If this shifting and contradictory wind of social change is a sign of anything, it is that these societies are going through profound changes because of the grave crisis they are experiencing. The crisis itself is a result of the conflict between traditional values and the hegemony and power of neo-imperialism, which increases not only the social and political isolation of these Arab societies from one another, but also the isolation and seclusion of women within these societies.

The debate about creativity and 'un-Islamic innovation', between modernization and tradition, and between emancipation and regression, is but a part of the general debate now going on in Arab society. It will continue to be an area of conflict until we arrive at an understanding of the laws and distinctive characteristics of Arab society in the neo-imperialist era.

The Family

It is not easy to make generalizations about the family in these societies because of the division which exists between the urban sector, which has undergone accelerated modernization, and the rural and bedouin sectors. None the less the incorporation of these societies into the capitalist market has strengthened the bonds between city and desert, creating sedentary tribal societies. Capitalist market relations have led to the formation of an embryonic class structure that assumes the outward form of kinship relations. Whereas the town, village, and desert used to be self-sufficient, these societies are now completely dependent on imported goods. There is no longer any need for society to produce, and women—like men, for that matter—have lost their old positions in production in towns, villages, and the desert areas. This has increased the traditional isolation of women, since society no longer requires their services in production. Even the most basic productive skills in traditional trades, agriculture, and handicrafts have begun to disappear, while the lure of consumerism, made possible by oil revenues, is assuming ever greater importance. One author, though perhaps overstating the case, has claimed:

> Work is not considered a sacred value as in other societies. The oil states are tending to become leisure societies handing out wages and allowances to the general public without demanding any work in return. This reduces the need to work and leads to large-scale absenteeism, evasion of responsibilities and duties, and abandonment of projects for no particular reason.[7]

The new economic system in the Gulf has prevented any active participation by society in the production of goods. This has led, among other things, to a downgrading of the position of women in the eyes of the majority of the population. Under the dependent 'extractive' and consumerist mode of production, a minority has come to control great wealth and power. Women of the ruling social classes are subservient to men, while the men of the middle and lower classes, deprived as they are of both wealth and power, are allowed to exercise control in just one area: over their women and children.

There is no longer any economic compulsion to have children, for the state now guarantees—and therefore controls—employment and pensions. A desire for male children nevertheless remains a very important feature of the Gulf family. Women feel socially and psychologically secure only if they have given birth to a son and heir. Family power is still measured by the number of sons. In order to retain wealth and power within the family, marriage (particularly among the upper classes) is restricted to paternal cousins. This has led to a decrease in the number of such families, and to a decline in their stock. More recently, men have accordingly been allowed to marry more distant relatives.

The situation has also led to difficult problems for women, who in modern society have tended to get married later or not at all. Education and their entrance into the work-force have exacerbated this problem. The first generation of educated women, whose fathers refused to marry them off to young men whom the family considered of a lower social status, paid what is a heavy price in this society, ending up as spinsters. Social factors themselves prevented the problem from being properly confronted.

Polygamy and divorce are important social phenomena in contemporary Gulf society. Polygamy is now less common than it was, particularly among the middle classes, although it remains widespread among both the bedouin and the super-rich (for different reasons). Whereas polygamy is becoming a relatively minor issue, the question of divorce is of wide concern. Both practices are male prerogatives. Most studies of divorce have concluded that its increase is a consequence of:

> socio-economic changes among the middle and upper-middle classes. Frequent disagreements arise between the wife and her mother-in-law, while the strong bonds between the husband and his family have a negative influence, leading to arguments between the mother and the wife.[8]

118

The study quoted above also reveals that divorcees have benefited from the opportunities for employment afforded by modern society. Divorce still causes considerable disruption, however. While the study deals only with Kuwaiti society, the difficulties faced by divorced women in the more traditional Gulf societies are even more extreme. The 'obedience' rules compel a divorced woman to live in a house provided for her by her husband, who is automatically granted custody of the children when they reach a certain age. Divorcees also have to endure social stigma, and are dependent on a male relative because of the social and psychological uncertainty resulting from any other course of action. This contrasts with the more traditional situation in which there is 'no stigma attached to divorce and it is not unusual for a woman to marry several times in her life, especially if she is from a good family or renowned for her beauty'.[9]

Marriage has become an economic problem as well. Since both men and women tend to marry later because of the new economic situation, the size of the average family has declined, and the difficulties of preparing for marriage (such as providing a house) have made marriage less common among the young. The state has now taken steps to provide financial incentives to encourage marriage and has imposed a legal limit on the value of dowries, the cost of which has soared as a result of the increased wealth, particularly among the upper classes. Large dowries have become a form of social ostentation, and staggering sums are often spent on wedding parties by the ignorant rich.

Some Gulf states have recently enacted laws which guarantee women equal wages for equal work, and accord certain rights to working women. These laws might seem progressive from the point of view of Western liberalism, but the usual situation pertains: it all depends on how such laws are applied, and a distinction between formal and real freedom persists. One study highlights the kind of contradiction that can exist even in the states that have taken notice of women's problems:

> We should note that even though women in Kuwait have the right to marry whoever they want, the personal status law stipulates that neither a young divorcee nor a previously unmarried woman may marry without the permission of the

father or grandfather.[10]

After discussion of the legal position of women in the Gulf, the study concludes:

> it is clear that much discrimination against women is still legally enshrined, particularly with regard to their political rights. Moreover, social customs and traditions, which have an important influence in the Gulf countries, have created a wide gap between the letter and the practice of the law.[11]

This is the situation prevailing in those countries in which legal stipulations are enshrined in a written constitution and in which various other laws have also been enacted. Yet the true rights of women are even more circumscribed in those countries which still lack any written laws governing relations between citizens.

The new economic situation has even given men additional means of isolating women. As one study notes, 'The effect of local traditions regarding sex segregation is still considerable [in the UAE], and no woman would embark on a career without first consulting her family, and the male head in particular.'[12] This comment might apply to virtually any woman in any Arab society.

Education and Labour

Let us bear in mind the caution voiced at the beginning of this chapter: it is simply not the case that an increase in female education and access to the labour market automatically brings an improvement in the social position of women, independently of general socio-economic and political conditions. It is true, however, that women are now being educated and are taking up paid employment in the Gulf countries, and the fact is not without importance. Table 4 shows how few women participate, or are allowed to participate, in the work-force. The figures reveal a further contradiction of Gulf societies: although labour is being imported (to the point that in some states more than half the population comes from outside the country and even from outside the Arab world), half the potential local work-force is excluded from the labour market. Here too the

Table 4: Working Women in the Gulf

	UAE	Bahrain	Oman	Qatar	Kuwait	Saudi Arabia
	1975	1971	1975	1975	1975	1975
Working women citizens as % of all workers	0.02	3.07	0.62	2.46	1.69	—
Working women citizens as % of all working citizens	1.06	4.87	3.03	3.66	8.52	2.01
Working women citizens as % of all working women	4.81	56.88	35.76	17.06	20.98	77.14
Immigrant working women as % of all workers	3.02	2.32	3.85	3.00	9.26	0.05
Immigrant working women as % of all immigrant workers	3.77	6.27	6.46	3.61	13.02	2.55

influence of the neo-traditionalists is apparent, for in the sixties and early seventies Gulf women played a more active role in the development of their countries. Subsequently there was less encouragement for women to work, partly because of neo-traditionalist pressure, and partly because of the economic situation.

The trend towards women working was purely formal in some Gulf societies, and was not based on any real economic need. Indeed, the richer these societies became, the less need there was. At a time when the state is providing substantial financial aid to widows and divorced women, and the neo-traditionalists are trying to promote the idea that a woman's work is in the home, there is less interest among women in the idea of work as a constructive socio-economic activity.

It is noteworthy that the number of workers (both men and women) employed as domestic servants continues to rise. This raises doubts that women are going back to their homes in order to look after the house and the children, and suggests that one reason why the population of the region continues to become more and more racially mixed is that workers are being imported as domestic servants.

The claim made by neo-traditionalists in other countries (such as Egypt) that working women deprive men of jobs has no credibility in the Gulf, for jobs there are both easy to come by and unproductive. Such people have therefore had to fall back on older ideas of modesty, seclusion, and the avoidance of 'un-Islamic' practices, even in those countries in which the socio-economic climate is favourable to women working. In Bahrain, for instance, there is a clear attempt to force women into isolation.

Because of the shortage of workers and the existence of un-employed indigenous surplus labour, the voices of those who support women's right to work are heard, even if only in certain economic sectors. Women are still educated to prepare them for certain selected forms of employment. Education is a very recent phenomenon, however. In countries like Saudi Arabia, Qatar, the UAE, and Oman the education of girls, in particular, began only in the sixties or seventies.

In 1981 Saudi Arabia celebrated the twentieth anniversary of the start of organized, official women's education. A report prepared for the occasion sets down the goals of women's education in the country:

the understanding of Islam, the establishment and propa-
gation of the Islamic faith in the hearts of the girls, and the
transmission of Islamic values and traditions. The characteristics of this system are derived from these goals.[13]

One requirement of this kind of education is that girls be taught by
women teachers. The Education Report goes on to say:

Studies have shown the importance of establishing crèches.
These would encourage those women who are already working
in education to carry on working; we should note, especially,
that many of the women employed in education who give up
their posts do so principally in order to look after their
children. On average, three women per day, both Saudi
nationals and contract teachers, give up their posts in primary
education.[14]

The problem here is that women have to be taught by other
women. If crèches are established, other women must be brought in
to staff them. There is no mixed education in Saudi Arabia; men are
forbidden to teach women, and women's education is a wholly
separate system. Moreover, Section Ten of the Saudi Arabian
Labour Code stipulates that men and women are forbidden to
associate with one another in any work-place or in any facility
or premises connected with work. In those few areas in which
circumstances had permitted such limited mixing of the sexes, the
authorities demanded that the companies concerned dismiss their
female employees and replace them by men.[15]

Women, however, make up half of society. They need to travel, for
example, and if circumstances demand, they have to be searched.
They have to buy clothes and household goods, and there must be
other women to sell them such things. Employing foreign women is a
temporary solution, even for the airlines, for it gives the impression
that two categories exist: local women who have to be secluded, and
foreign women who can be employed anywhere! Certain sectors of
society therefore require female labour. But any attempt to interpret
the position of women in the Gulf solely in terms of the labour-
market would lead to serious misunderstanding. The mere fact that
women are employed in the police force, or as broadcasters, teachers,

or even in the armed forces by no means signifies the emancipation of Arab Gulf women. True emancipation can be achieved only through solving the basic problems of society.

The new economic situation in the Gulf has accelerated the pace of change. This has had both positive and negative effects on the position of women. It is an over-simplification to say that the issue concerns modernization versus tradition, or liberation versus narrow-minded religiosity. One of the facts that emerges from the discussion here is that some phenomena disappear only to re-emerge, which means that no complete or radical solution to the problems they reflected had ever been found. The superficial, 'modern' liberation of women turned out to be a bubble that soon burst. Fundamentally, the political status of women remains what it always has been. Women's labour and education have been limited to particular spheres of activity and to fields of study decreed by society. Their social and political freedom is similarly restricted. If women are to be truly liberated and to participate in the development of the Arab nation, there must be radical social change of a type still feared by the ruling classes. These classes are now adopting various means to prevent such change, including the modern media, and pressure groups set up by the neo-traditionalists. They are promoting the idea that women are excessively emotional beings, both respected and feared by men, who thus have to keep them in seclusion.

9
Citizens and Immigrant Workers

There is little reliable information about immigrant workers in the Gulf countries, most of which keep no precise statistics of general demographic and social questions and sometimes no statistics at all. Moreover, the social and political effects of the massive immigrant presence depend not only on the relations between population groups, but also on the perception of those relations, whether accurate or not.

Local and Immigrant Labour

Lack of balance in the labour market is one of the major problems caused by the type of development experienced by the Gulf countries in the sixties and seventies. These countries concentrated mainly on building roads and ports, expanding education, and establishing medical institutions and a host of other essential projects. Investment mushroomed in the first half of the seventies, especially after the rise in oil prices. Because of the weakness of the local work-force and the shortage of available labour, immigrants began to flow in to run these expanded services. This immigration was partly spontaneous and partly organized. The immigrants came from a number of culturally heterogeneous regions and from various parts of the Arab world.

The original immigration dates back to the years just after the Second World War, when the immigrants came mainly from the Indian subcontinent. Under colonial rule immigrants were granted certain privileges denied the local workers. This gave rise to conflict between the two groups. Western oil companies, which had direct or indirect control over many of the internal decisions taken by these countries, were slow to respond to the demands of local workers. In the fifties, when the new service projects began, the state used non-local labour, a policy that has continued to the present day.

Various groups in Gulf society warned of the dangers of such immigration, in particular from non-Arab sources, but these warnings were not heeded. In the past few years, semi-official bodies have shown some concern about the large numbers of people of foreign origin now resident in the Gulf. But there are objective reasons why the problem of foreign workers will be a long-term one. In the absence of any co-ordinated regional plan, there is little hope of a solution in the foreseeable future.

The Gulf countries got rich so fast and were incorporated into the world capitalist market so suddenly that no radical changes in social structure accompanied their economic expansion. This expansion is based on the export of a single commodity and the import of almost everything else, from matches to motor cars. Most of the problems faced by immigrant workers, whether Arab or foreign, arise from the socio-political structures of these countries as they are hurled, in sensitive global circumstances, from tribalism to 'cosmopolitan' conditions. Development plans require structural socio-cultural changes, but present cultural patterns are based on the traditional social structure. This is the heart of the problem.

All the signs are that the influx of foreign labour will increase in coming years. Moreover, there is likely to be a higher proportion of Asians than Arabs among the immigrants, partly because the Arab labour-market is unable to provide the increasing numbers of workers required, and partly because the Asian workers possess the relatively advanced technical skills now needed.[1] The attitude of Gulf governments to the problem of immigrant labour has been accurately described as 'pragmatism of an ever-changing and frequently self-contradictory type'.[2]

The situation is increasingly dangerous. The large number of people from different ethnic backgrounds threatens the identity of the region. Rules and laws are applied to the immigrants that are, at the very least, inhumane. This generates great bitterness among the immigrant workers. There are also negative sentiments among the local population. Arab and non-Arab immigrants are present in all the Gulf states. In Saudi Arabia and Kuwait the majority of immigrants are Arabs, whereas in Bahrain, Qatar and the UAE most are non-Arabs. The Arab immigrants come mostly from the eastern part of the Arab world, including Egypt. Few are from North Africa. Arab immigrants are employed as administrative officials in both the government and private sectors, especially in positions that require a facility in Arabic, like teaching and management. They also take skilled, semi-skilled, and unskilled jobs. The Arab immigration pre-dates the oil boom. There was an influx of Palestinians after the 1948 disaster, and many of the early immigrants were Egyptians. Iraqi educational missions had also been established. Arab immigration increased when the newly independent Gulf states relaxed the restrictions of the colonial era. But the heaviest migrations came in the sixties and seventies.

Today there are Arab families in the Gulf who have lived there for three or more generations; many of their number have spent their entire adult lives 'in the service of the Arab society' to which they emigrated. Most of the children of these families were born in the Gulf countries and have been educated in the same schools as the sons and daughters of the local inhabitants. At first, Arab immigrants were welcomed by the local people, although certain sections of the local societies were somewhat apprehensive as the general culture of the immigrant Arabs differed from that of the local population in some respects: they wore Western clothes, ate different foods, and spoke a different dialect of Arabic. But in general they were seen to be performing useful services in the new schools and hospitals and in the administration, where qualified local personnel were lacking.

As the independent Gulf states developed, however, difficulties for Arab immigrants mounted, both in terms of gaining admittance to the country and in terms of employment and legal status. It is ironic that some groups of Arab immigrants were themselves partially responsible for presenting a generally favourable picture of the discriminatory legal treatment of immigrants. It was usually the Arab immigrants in government service who actually drafted the new laws dealing with immigration, residence, employment, education, and so on. With the undoubted complicity of those responsible for decision-making in the fifties, sixties, and even seventies, these people strove to present the institutionalization of discrimination against immigrants in a favourable light.

In part this may have been a consequence of the nature of Gulf society itself. Ibrahim al-Ibrahim has commented:

> The Gulf is still at a stage where the group takes precedence over the individual . . . In the Gulf, the whole is more than a group of individuals each of whom has equal rights and duties. Even now, personal status and position in society continue to be measured by social background and tribal lineage.[3]

He concludes that only open societies can welcome immigrants.

There are other factors too, however. The financial surplus enjoyed by these societies as a result of oil has linked them to the centres of modern capitalism, to the states of the industrialized world. It is in the interest of these states to deal with small, weak countries that possess neither productive nor political independence so that they remain dependent on Western industries and Western protection, incapable of taking positive decisions about oil prices, production levels, or the way oil revenues are used. Thus these societies' isolation also reduces the power of Arab nationalism and prevents the region taking its proper place in the international arena as a rich, powerful, and unified bloc. The discrimination that exists is therefore the result not only of internal socio-economic structures but also of external links to the industrialized states. Despite the general sentiments of Arab 'harmony' among Arabs living in the region and the sense of shared common goals, secondary tensions between the local people and the Arab immigrants continue to exist below the surface.

The initial reaction of local people to Arab immigration was not 'hostile', though it was cautious. Gradually, however, it became somewhat less than friendly. As educational levels among the local inhabitants rose, they found that many administrative posts (the major source of employment) were occupied by Arab immigrants. This generated a hidden conflict. The differences between immigrant and local Arabs were aggravated because the former had come from many different areas. Immigrants from Egypt, with its long bureaucratic tradition, met 'opposition' from both local inhabitants and Arabs from Greater Syria. Conflict emerged between the various Arab communities, each of which sought to obtain jobs and to monopolize particular areas of work. Political divisions among the

Arab immigrants were also a factor: 'progressive' Arabs were viewed with suspicion by the regimes, which tried to suppress their opinions, while conservative Arabs were mistrusted by local Arab nationalist forces.

The authorities enacted laws and regulations to reduce the degree of contact between immigrant Arabs and the local inhabitants. Non-Gulf Arabs were ordered to live in blocks of flats segregated from the dwellings of local people. Relations between them were limited to work-places, and social and family relations declined. It is also worth noting that social interaction between the various Arab immigrant groups—Egyptians, Syrians, Palestinians, and so on—was limited, the members of each group normally associating with their compatriots alone. Moreover, political disagreements in other parts of the Arab world had repercussions on the Arabs living in the Gulf. The Camp David agreement and Egypt's subsequent withdrawal from the ranks of Arab states had a markedly negative effect on relations between Egyptians and other Arab immigrants. Negative feelings between Syrians and Palestinians also emerged whenever conflict occurred between the two groups elsewhere.

The degree to which people from the various Arab countries associate with one another also depends on economic and professional status. There are markedly close relations between social groups of high cultural standing, and similarly close relations between those of a lower cultural level, such as unskilled workers. But there is a clear gap between the two groups. Professionals such as doctors, engineers, and university lecturers share common interests and live in close proximity in specially designated accommodation. This is also true of workers employed on the same site. The gap between the inhabitants of different Arab countries is greater among groups of average educational and economic status, such as middle-ranking government workers and officials. Here the most obvious factor is competition: each group seeks to present a more favourable picture of its own work to its superiors, the department head normally being a local citizen.

Immigrant workers from all Arab countries generally present both Arabs from other countries and local Arab inhabitants as lazy, hypocritical, indifferent and snobbish. This is one result of the fierce competition for jobs in the public and private sector alike. Immigrant Arabs generally have a negative and distorted image of the local Arab population, regarding them as unproductive, arrogant, concerned only with making money, and uninterested in human or cultural questions.

Top posts in the oil states are reserved exclusively for local people, regardless of their experience or qualifications. Similarly, local people are normally paid more than foreign or Arab immigrant workers. The figures for Kuwait displayed in Table 5 are illustrative.

Table 5: Average Monthly Earnings (Kuwaiti Dinars)

Scale	Kuwaitis	Non-Kuwaitis
0	239	206
1	251	190
2	556	503
3	189	185
4	253	200
5	162	80
6	191	69
7	220	106
8	202	63
9	189	67

Source: 'An Observer: Oil for Underdevelopment and Discrimination: The case of Kuwait', *Monthly Review*, vol. 30, no. 6, Nov. 1978, p. 21.

Local authorities justify such wage differentials by claiming that they represent a form of assistance to citizens, who for many years were denied reasonable incomes or comfortable life-styles. Others argue that they have detrimental effects on both public- and private-sector companies. They also argue that local people already benefit from housing, education, and other services that are provided free to citizens. Such privileges, they say, are sufficient and should not be supplemented by higher wages.

Labour legislation in the Gulf countries discriminates between local and immigrant workers, both foreign and Arab. Laws on such matters as female labour, industrial accidents, and workers' rights sometimes conflict with international labour agreements that these countries have themselves signed. These laws prohibit immigrant Arab workers from joining trade unions, so that even if such unions are not actually banned, their membership is restricted to local people. Labour legislation provides no guarantees whatever for the Arab worker. Other labour laws not only infringe the rights of Arab workers, but also exclude those employed in the police and defence forces, on the grounds that such people are vital to the national interest.

Some immigrant Arabs have had an influence on the local political scene both directly and indirectly. Recent political legislation in the Gulf—such as laws relating to the press and education—has generally been produced by Arab consultants. Unofficial political influence has been far-reaching and was particularly important in the fifties and early sixties in Kuwait, when the Arab nationalist movement was active throughout the Arab world. Both local and immigrant Arabs were involved in political gatherings and seminars. Organized political activities by immigrant Arabs began to arouse the concern of the local authorities, however, particularly when they were linked to those of the local population. A hard-line attitude was taken with regard to Arabs involved in local political questions and a number of people were deported.

The Influence of Non-Arab Immigrants

There probably never was a time when the Arab Gulf was inhabited exclusively by Arabs. Because of the region's proximity to Iran, India, and Africa, there were always migrations even before the discovery of oil. Sunni Muslims from Iran, for instance, came fleeing persecution, particularly in the twenties and thirties. The favourable economic situation after the Second World War attracted a new wave of migration from Iran. Well before oil, Indian merchants acted as middlemen and purchasing agents for local products, in particular pearls, which they then sold on the Indian and world markets. Families from India and Iran settled in the Gulf countries, and a few—particularly those who arrived before the discovery of oil— were assimilated into local society. These early Persian and Indian migrations had only limited effects on the local society. Although these immigrant cultures absorbed much local culture and tradition, there was no profound social intermixing and no intermarriage. Ultimately, the majority of the immigrants were not assimilated.

The new migrations after the Second World War came from the same areas, Iran and India. This time, however, larger numbers of people were involved, and the immigrants found employment not as merchants but in the oil industry and in government and economic posts that required a knowledge of English. Indians also worked in the service sector, sometimes in low-status jobs like laundering, tailoring, and domestic service. Some of the Indians moved into the retail trade, where they were often highly successful, but the majority worked on building sites and in service areas, some of which they monopolized, such as baking, and cargo-handing in the expanding ports.

These immigrants groups were subject to the same laws as the Arab workers, and like the Arabs were debarred from organizing themselves. Because of their relatively comfortable life-style compared with the conditions they had fled, they generally maintained and respected local customs. Their language shows a marked influence of eastern Arabic dialects, and it is not uncommon for an observer coming across a group of workers speaking in Syrian dialect to discover that they are actually from Iran or India. In the seventies, immigration from Iran dried up and these groups began returning home, since work there was now becoming more readily available.

Neither of these groups of immigrants has had a great deal of political influence, that of the Indians being particularly small. In the fifties, sixties, and much of the seventies, the traditional hostility between Arabs and Iranians was fuelled by the Shah's imperial ambitions and by his government's repeated claims to sovereignty over several islands in the Gulf, including Bahrain. This had negative effects on relations between the local Arabs and Iranians, the former viewing the latter as a kind of fifth column of the Shah's army. Indeed, some Iranians made no secret of their feelings on the matter, and several Iranian mercantile groups had interests that coincided with the Shah's imperial designs, a factor that aggravated the suspicions of the local Arabs.

In more recent years, however, internal developments in Iran, the increasing precariousness of Iranian armed control of the Gulf, and the return of large numbers of Iranians to Iran have led to a decrease in the feelings of hostility and political apprehension that have traditionally existed between local Gulf Arabs and the Iranians living among them.

In the past ten years the Gulf has seen a huge influx of Asian immigrant workers from lands east of the subcontinent, in particular Korea and the Philippines. This immigration is now highly organized, and the large numbers of people involved are housed in special work camps that have been set up to handle them. However, it has also been a source of extreme apprehension and heated debate among the local population. The authorities justify the importation of these workers from South-East Asia on the grounds that they are needed to carry through the enormous projects now planned. But local Arabs feel that these workers might in the future be used as a kind of reserve army with which to occupy the whole region. The question of Asian workers is a burning issue in the Gulf press.

The Gulf countries face the prospect of a rising demand for foreign workers. At the same time, the harsh laws against them have segregated these immigrant workers, turning them into machines rather than working-class families. The structure of the Gulf societies dictated the adoption of certain measures and decisions designed to protect these societies, or certain sectors of them, from the social and political influence of the immigrant workers. The immigrant communities, however, are themselves taking steps to gain a foothold in local political affairs. The future will probably see demands from both nationalist and humanitarian forces among the local inhabitants that the immigrants be granted general rights. National, regional, and international institutions have begun to demand an improvement in the conditions of immigrant workers.

A large proportion of the local Arab population has reacted to the immigrants, especially the Asians, with doubt and misgiving. The problem of immigrant workers is but one element in the whole issue of the development policies pursued by these countries.

10
From Dependency to Independence

During the three decades that followed the Second World War the economic structures of the Gulf countries were transformed by oil. In those areas in which oil was discovered late or not at all its advent was nevertheless awaited breathlessly, for the transformation of economic life through oil revenues represented the hope of an escape from subsistence. The mass of the population increasingly abandoned their traditional economic pursuits and were drawn into activities that depended on oil revenues.[1]

The new dependence on oil resembled the traditional dependence on pastoralism, agriculture, and pearl-diving in that both the pre-capitalist and the capitalist modes of production were at the mercy of 'nature'. There was no gradual expansion of internal productive forces, and the impetus behind the new mode of production was not indigenous development but Western capitalist technology. The economic activities of the oil industry were completely separate from the distribution of oil revenues. This contradiction lies at the heart of the current social situation in the Gulf states. At the start of the oil boom, the tribe was the basic social unit. Although the political role of the tribe was later restricted, some of its formal aspects were retained to preserve those traditional social relations which bolstered the political structure. The emergence of a single ruling family or clan from among the various other families, tribes, and clans was facilitated by that family's control of the new wealth. The pace of change quickened, but all the changes were ambiguous, as the new wealth encouraged certain trends already latent in the Gulf societies. The ensuing structural transformations may be summarized under three headings: urbanization and population shifts; cultural and educational change; political change.

Urbanization and Population Shifts

The extent and pace of urbanization in the Gulf countries have been unprecedented. When Bahrain first began producing oil in the mid-thirties, there was an influx of immigrants from the interior into the settled regions, and from beyond the surrounding area into Bahrain. The same thing later happened in Kuwait, Qatar, the UAE, and Saudi Arabia. In these cases, however, the numbers involved were much greater, the origins of the immigrants more diverse.

The migration from agricultural lands and the desert to the cities has been so sweeping that Bahrain, Qatar, and Kuwait have become entirely urbanized, possibly even over-urbanized. When inhabitants of the countryside or the desert leave their homes for the modern towns, they abandon their traditional economic life permanently, settling for good in the places they find jobs.

Large sections of the people who flocked to the cities abandoned their former crafts and sought work in the modern economic sectors, but since many of them lacked the ability to do skilled or even semi-skilled work, a broad belt of what might be called 'bedouin-proletarians' sprang up around the towns. In this context, some states pursued apparently contradictory goals, trying to maintain traditional economic sectors such as agriculture and fishing, while simultaneously taking measures to facilitate participation by the local population in the new economic sectors. This contradiction has prevented full utilization of either the land or human resources. The subsidies earmarked for agriculture have been used to buy modern consumer goods in the cities instead.

Cultural and Educational Change

One of the chief features of the Gulf societies is their youth: the majority of the local population are under 15 years old. Large amounts of money have been spent on education, which now consumes a greater proportion of resources than any other area. The third post-oil generation now studying or being trained may be of fundamental importance in the incorporation of local people into the modern economic sector.

Although the progress made in education has been a source of great satisfaction to some, it has proved a disappointment to others, for the goals of educational planning have been primarily quantitative, qualitative aspects being largely ignored.

Nevertheless, education has undoubtedly provided an opportunity for reshaping society—educated people have taken up public posts and some have received advanced training in the modern economic sectors. Expenditure on radio and television has also provided a channel for disseminating concepts about health and society; the media have thus played a subsidiary role in communicating modern ideas to the population. Moreover, the facts of modern economic life have forced many sections of society to take an interest in culture.

Education has produced many specialists in theory, but people have generally been discouraged from pursuing technical or vocational education. Moreover, because of the ease with which the local inhabitants are able to find jobs, many people have contented themselves with the minimum of education. Many young people give up school to take up some form of paid employment that will allow them to participate in the consumer society.

There are those who hope that education will ultimately create a new consciousness. One author has remarked in this regard:

> It may well be that education itself and the kind of consciousness arising from it and from cultural contact with the outside world—which may be the most important positive effect of current changes—represent the main hope for the continued development of the countries of the region.[2]

But present methods of education are unlikely to create the sort of consciousness that would lead to the establishment of a productive base and diversification of the income sources unless some deliberate political choices are made.

Political Change

The oil industry and its multinational companies have forged close links between the Gulf countries and the Western market and Western governments. Indeed, some people have described the local political ruling groups as functionaries administering the Gulf societies on behalf of the international bourgeoisie.

This is perhaps an over-statement of the realities of the socio-economic situation and it does not fully explain the present transitional stage. Some political modernization has in fact occurred, and it is doubtful if this transitional phase can be frozen indefinitely. If sharp contradictions between the socio-economic and political structures arise, an explosion could result. The economic and social aspects of modernization will inevitably find some corresponding political expression eventually. On the other hand, there may shortly be some deliberate steps towards political modernization. Many promises have been made that a political administration will be established in which ministers are appointed on the basis of specialist and technical qualifications. But formal changes will not be enough. Apart from the general problem of development, political transformation is the most fundamental issue now faced by these societies. The present political regimes will survive only if they solve it.

Characteristics of the Social Structure

The major features of the consumer society that now prevails in the Gulf have become more apparent with every rise in oil revenues. It is the ruling clan—in the form of the state—that acts as principal distributor of oil income. This is reflected in both social relations and political institutions. On the one hand, oil revenues have enabled the state to expand the infrastructure, which has brought fundamental changes in social structures. On the other hand, the state has kept ultimate power of decision in the hands of the tribe. So far the contradiction has been contained, because the motive force of the society is not production but the distribution of revenue by the state; actual production of oil is carried out entirely by foreigners, the local population playing a virtually insignificant role in the productive process.

Such factors as financial subsidies, loans, government projects, urbanization, and the destruction of the old quarters of towns might have been expected to bring about a rapid collapse of the tribal system. In the Gulf, however, it is the tribal system itself that forms the basis for all forms of 'assistance', such as appointment to government posts, entry into the police or armed forces, or state expenditure on the civilian sector, through merchants and contractors. This system creates two basic social classes.

The dominant class, which controls the consumption and internal distribution of durable and non-durable commodities, is linked to the industrialized countries; it is basically led by a mercantile capitalist group that pre-dates the oil era and has grown rich through contracting and the import of goods. It has two components, which have common interests but a different social status: the old-established merchant groups and the new rich. Both sections of this class are involved in contracting, real estate, and speculation on the stock exchange, as well as banking, insurance, and transportation. The members of this class are to be found in the towns of both the interior and the coast. They have close connections with the ruling clan, and are sometimes members of the same tribe. Their numbers are small relative to the other social sub-classes. During the fifties and sixties the dominant class supported demands for political participation and opposed direct colonialism. In the seventies, however, its growing wealth and its links to international capital led it to oppose popular demands.

The second social class—direct consumers—may also be divided into two sub-groups. The first consists of top and middle-ranking government employees and retail merchants; the second is made up of low-ranking government employees, the urban poor (the bedouin-proletariat), artisans, local unskilled workers, and skilled and unskilled immigrant workers. It is this class whose dependence on the consumption of imported goods assures the perpetuation of the present social formation.

All these groups demand increases in consumption, which necessarily leads to dependence on Western sources of production. But they also have other ambitions that run counter to this trend. The class that controls consumption, for instance—in particular the mercantile capitalists—seeks higher profits both inside and outside the region. They thus favour industrialization: the establishment of new conversion industries, a concentration of capital in productive industry, a reduction in the number of immigrant workers, a monopoly on import concessions, and an important role for their own members in joint government and private-sector companies. These demands generally accord with those of the direct consumer class, though there is sometimes conflict here. The controlling class, for example, would favour a reduction in the number of foreign workers, but also supports increased reliance on them because their labour is cheap, they are unprotected by labour laws, they rent houses and flats that are owned by this class, and they purchase their consumer goods from such members of this class as car-dealers and retailers of household goods.

The Gulf societies are based on a dichotomy between the production of oil on the one hand and the wealth generated by this production on the other. They are held together by a tripartite alliance of the conservative authorities (the ruling clan), the owners of commercial capital, and the top layers of the educated elite. The people of the Gulf are generally divorced from production: they are the recipients of wealth but not its creators. Mercantile capital benefits directly from the present form of growth, and the entire system is administered by an educated elite that wants a share of the wealth it sees around it. An individual's value in this society derives from his relation to the authorities, the ruling family. People are given what they need and are supposed to show gratitude for what they get. They are treated as 'subjects' (subject to the protection of others). The result has been a mentality that even the Saudi minister of industry has condemned as based on four myths: that the Gulf countries have an inexhaustible supply of money; that money itself can solve all problems; that any problem can be dealt with by establishing a new administrative body; that development can be imported wholesale in the form of equipment, contractors, technical experts, and workers.[3]

In the expanding cities of the Gulf, oil revenues have given rise to groups of contractors and mercantile capitalists who have been supported by the ruling class through the generous provision of state loans and facilities. Some of these groups are demanding an expansion of the Gulf market and a share in the political process. In several states they have registered some success, while in others they remain entirely excluded from politics. In parts of the region, this merchant bourgeoisie has been able to push through legal measures to eliminate foreign competition and has built up local economic sectors such as banking and insurance. Elsewhere it has entered into partnership with foreign interests, taking a majority stake of 51 per cent. Over the coming ten years these activities will lead to an increase in economic weight at the expense of foreign interests, and the removal from the Gulf market of the remnants of foreign banks, insurance companies, and merchants. These indigenous groups will also try to gain a share of political power and to obtain legislation regulating the foreign work-force.

Industrial conversion products will also be set up to provide for the needs of the local market. There are, however, certain obstacles. The administration will have to be modernized, to achieve greater flexibility and competence. The current bureaucratic apparatus has led to a rise in administrative corruption. This originally took hold when these societies were poor, and has spread because of the lack of effective controls, the interplay of family interests, and the enormous increase in the size of the apparatus itself. The political and social integration of the various conflicting groups requires a strategy and an ideology which stress the concepts of patriotism, equality of opportunity, and the just application of the law to all groups. A clear decision on political participation is a prerequisite for this.

Ideological changes are also required, in particular the introduction of secular ideas in place of supernatural interpretations of events. This can be achieved only through cultural programmes that are in harmony with the aims and methods of modernization. Such programmes would face many practical difficulties. Modern educational programmes designed to provide effective practical training in construction, commerce, services, and industry are equally necessary.

Social justice, efficient production and organization, and—even more fundamentally—individual awareness of such matters face opposition from vested interests, both internally and externally. Some of the groups in these societies that benefit from the present situation view with discomfort any possibility of national merger or even integration with neighbouring Gulf countries. These forces continue to block any rational or open political development.

Notes

Chapter 1

1. Pearl-diving is mentioned in classical Arab works, the most famous examples being references by Ibn Battuta, and by the well-known historian al-Mas'udi in his book *The Golden Meadows*. See Saif Marzuq al-Shamlan, *The History of Pearl-Diving in Kuwait and the Arabian Peninsula*, Part ɪ, Kuwait 1975; Part ɪɪ, Kuwait 1978.

2. Stanley Mallory, *Kuwait Before Oil*.

3. The financing of the whole project was also called the *taqasum*. This was a loan from the merchants to the ship's captain, as J. G. Lorimer informs us in his *Gazetteer of the Persian Gulf*, Historical Section, Part ᴠɪ, pp. 20–32: 'But those who do not have sufficient capital borrow the necessary money from the big Arab traders'—or from Indian merchants at an interest rate of 10–25 per cent for a single season.

4. For a more detailed discussion of relations in the pearl industry see a number of essays by Khalifa Turki al-Rashid entitled 'A Cry from the Past to the Present', Kuwait undated.

5. See, for instance, the Law on Divers in Kuwait, which was promulgated in Kuwait in 1940: al-Shamlan, *History of Pearl-Diving*, Part ɪɪ, p. 104.

6. Muhammad Abdu Mahjub, *Migration and Changes in Social Structure in Kuwaiti Society*, D. T. Publications Agency, Kuwait, undated, pp. 120ff.

7. See Yusif Ibn Isa al-Qina'i, *Pages from the History of Kuwait*, 4th edn, Kuwait 1968, p. 86.

8. Muhammad Ghanim al-Rumaihi, *Problems of Social and Political Change in Bahrain*, Beirut 1976, Part ɪᴠ, ch. 1.

9. Abdallah Zakariya al-Ansari, *Fahd the Soldier* (Introduction to 3rd edn, 1972).

10. Mahjub, *Migration and Changes*, p. 115.

11. Al-Qina'i, *Pages from the History of Kuwait*, p. 78.

12. Mallory, *Kuwait Before Oil*, pp. 12ff.

13. For details of the pearl-diving law in Kuwait, see al-Shamlan, *History of Pearl-Diving*. This law was promulgated on 29 May 1940.

14. Al-Qina'i, *Pages from the History of Kuwait*.

15. Amin al-Raihani, *The Arab Kings*, 5th edn, Beirut 1968, Part II, pp. 172–3.

16. Ibid., p. 286. It is known that al-Raihani visited the Gulf emirates in the 1920s. He describes what he witnessed during that period.

17. On the subject of education in Kuwait, see Badr al-Din Abbas al-Kushusi, *Studies in the Economic and Social History of Kuwait*, Kuwait 1972, ch. 1. For Bahrain, see al-Rumaihi, *Problems of Social Change*.

Chapter 2

1. On this subject see Ahmad Mustafa Abu Hakma, *History of Kuwait*, Kuwait 1970.

2. There are many examples of how the British persistently tried to fragment the Gulf through treaties with Ibn Saud, particularly the Treaty of Jeddah, 1927. Britain pursued the same aim through various conferences which were held to demarcate borders. The most famous of these was the Uqair conference of 1922, at which the Kuwaiti, Saudi, and Iraqi borders were drawn up under direct British supervision. For further details, see Husayn M. al-Baharna, *The Legal Status of the Arabian Gulf States: A Study of their Treaty Relations and their International Problems*, Manchester 1968.

3. See, for instance, Clarence C. Mann, *Abu Dhabi, Birth of an Oil Sheikhdom*, Beirut 1969.

4. See H. R. P. Dickson, *The Arab of the Desert: A Basic Map of the Tribal Lands of Mutair*.

5. Muhammad Ahmad Abd al-Ati, 'Political Development in Kuwait', unpublished dissertation, supervised by al-Ahram Centre for Political and Strategic Studies, Cairo.

6. See the important discussion by Nazih Abu Nidal, in which he argues against the view that there are different Arab races and nationalities (*Journal of Arab Studies*, no. 3, Year 14, Jan. 1978, pp. 92–116), particularly with regard to the role of the common economic factor in the building of national identity.

7. On this topic, see Futuh Abd al-Muhsin al-Khatrash, *The History of Anglo-Kuwaiti Political Relations, 1890–1921*, Kuwait 1974, especially the chapter on Anglo-Kuwaiti relations and their effects on Saudi-Kuwaiti relations, pp. 87–117.

8. Khalid al-Sa'dun Jasim, 'Factors Affecting the Balance of Revenue Distribution: A Study of Kuwait', *Journal of Gulf and Peninsula Studies*, Oct. 1977.

9. For further details on this topic, see the valuable study by Dr Ali Khalifa al-Kawari, *Oil Revenues in the Gulf Emirates*, Durham 1974, particularly ch. 18.

Chapter 3

1. The term 'Gulf countries', used in this chapter to refer to the oil-producing countries of the Arabian peninsula, refers principally to the six members of the Gulf Co-operation Council.

2. There have been a number of works on this topic. See, for instance, Dr Mahmoud Abd al-Fadil, *Oil and Contemporary Problems of Arab Growth*, World of Knowledge Series, Kuwait April 1979, p. 204.

3. Dr Ghazi al-Qusaibi, *Facing Development*, Jeddah 1981, p. 40.

4. For details, see Dr Ali al-Kawari, 'Facts About Oil Development: the Case of the Countries of the Arabian Peninsula', *Journal of the Arab Future*, no. 27, May 1981, p. 36.

5. For this analysis, see John G. Taylor, *From Modernization to Modes of Production. A Critique of the Sociologies of Development and Under-Development*, Atlantic Highlands, New Jersey 1979.

6. Abd al-Aziz Abdallah al-Zamil, 'Why Industrialization in the Arabian Peninsula?', unpublished lecture given as part of the Development Studies Project for the Countries of the Gulf in Doha (Qatar), April 1972.

7. Ibid., p. 4.

8. Ahmad Zaki al-Yamani, 'Oil and Money in the Eighties', paper presented at the Second Colloquium on Oil and Money, organized by the *Herald Tribune*, London, September 1981.

9. Askari and Jalal, 'The Role and Management of Current Account Surpluses in the Oil-Producing Countries of the Arabian Peninsula', unpublished paper presented at the Colloquium on Gulf Development, March 1983, p. 16.

10. Al-Qusaibi, *Facing Development*.

11. Ibid.

12. See the unpublished study undertaken by the Industrial Consultancy Office, 'Reports on the Results of the General Inquiry into Activities in the Conversion Industries in Some of the States of the Gulf Co-operation Council', p. 28.

13. Abd al-Fadil, *Oil and Contemporary Problems*, p. 105.

14. Askari and Jalal, 'Role and Management of Current Account Surpluses', p. 61.

15. Ibid., p. 95.

16. On this topic, see a series of studies presented to the Colloquium on Foreign Labour in the Countries of the Gulf, organized by the Study Centre for Arab Unity and held in Kuwait, 15–18 Jan. 1983.

17. Nadir al-Farajani, 'The Size and Composition of the Work-Force in the Gulf', *The Arab Future*, no. 50, April 1973, p. 70.

18. Muhammad Abd al-Rahman al-Tawil, 'Towards the Creation of a Local Administrative Leadership for Development', unpublished lecture given as part of the Development Studies Project for the Countries of the Gulf in Doha (Qatar), March 1982, p. 10.

19. On this subject, see the important study by Isama Abd al-Rahman,

'Oil Bureaucracy and the Problem of Development', in *World of Knowledge*, National Council for Culture, Arts, and Humanities, Kuwait, no. 57, Sept. 1982.

20. For details see the valuable study by Ali al-Kawari, 'The Role of Public Projects in Economic Development', *World of Knowledge*, no. 43, June 1981, p. 195.

Chapter 4

1. Quoted from a public lecture to Higher Studies students at Durham University (UK), in 1973, after Sir Arthur had resigned from his post. This lecture was attended by the author.

2. Hussein Muhammad al-Baharna, *The Modern Gulf States: Their International Relations and the Development of their Political, Legal and Constitutional Positions*, Beirut 1973, p. 41.

3. Ibid., p. 45.

4. Riyadh al-Rayyis, *Oil and the Conflict Between the Oases*, p. 12.

5. Jamal Zakariya Qasim, 'Trends Towards Unification in the Gulf Region', International Colloquium of the Centre for Third World Studies, 29–31 March 1979; *Man and Society in the Countries of the Gulf*, Basra 1979.

6. Some contemporary historians such as Zakariya Qasim and Ahmad Abu Hakima also place the Al Sa'ud in the Atub alliance. It is generally agreed, however, that the Al Sa'ud bear no relation to this alliance. See Hamad al-Jasir, 'The History of Kuwait', *Journal of Gulf and Peninsula Studies*, no. 6, April 1976.

7. The term 'Prohibition Agreements' refers to the treaties Britain imposed on the Gulf sheikhs in the 1880s and 1890s. The treaties prevented the sheikhs from exercising independent control over their lands and from entering into negotiations with any other power.

8. See the text referred to in note 2, above.

9. For details, see *Middle East Journal*, vol. 1, 1947; vol. 2, 1948; vol. 9, 1955; vol. 10, 1956.

10. For details see Muhammad Ghanim al-Rumaihi, *Problems of Social and Political Change in Bahrain*, Beirut 1976, Part III, ch. 1.

11. Rosemarie Said Zahlan, *The Origins of the United Arab Emirates. A Political and Social History of the Trucial States*, London 1978, pp. 102–03.

12. Abu Khaldun Sati' al-Hassari, 'On Arab Unity', *The Arab Future*, no. 10, Nov. 1979, pp. 114–23, in which the author refers to studies of a secret document dated 13 June 1933, produced by the British government under the title 'The Attitude of His Majesty's Government to the Question of Arab Unity'. This document concludes that Gulf unity ran counter to the interests of the British government.

13. Amin al-Raihani, *The Arab Kings,* 5th edn, Beirut 1968, Part II, p. 267.

14. Rosemarie Said Zahlan, 'Leadership, Independence and Development in the Gulf', paper presented at the Colloquium on Economic and Social Development Strategies in the Gulf, Exeter (UK), 9–13 July 1979, p. 9.

15. Al-Rayyis, *Oil and the Conflict Between the Oases*, p. 34.

16. Ibid., p. 99.

17. Al-Baharna, *Modern Gulf States*, app. 5, p. 204.

18. For further details, see: Muhammad Rashid al-Ril, 'Border Problems between the Gulf Emirates', *Journal of Gulf and Peninsula Studies*, no. 8, pp. 25 and 64; Abdallah al-Ash'al, *Border Questions in the Arab World*, Publications Series no. 28, Cairo 1978, ch. 2.

19. The British position before the Second World War was to oppose all forms of Arab unity, including any kind of union between the Gulf emirates, or in the southern half of Yemen. On this subject see the important document discussed by al-Hassari (see note 12 above).

20. On this subject, see: al-Sayyid Muhammad Ibrahim, *The Bases of Political and Constitutional Organization in the United Arab Emirates*, Abu Dhabi 1975, pp. 50–1; Abd al-Rahman Ghanim and Muhammad Ibrahim al-Sha'ir, *The National Strategy of the United Arab Emirates*, Damascus 1978.

21. See the legal study by Uthman Abd al-Malik concerning the legal status of Gulf companies, in *al-Watan*, Kuwaiti daily newspaper, November 1979. The article contains a detailed discussion of some of the articles of the constitution of the UAE.

22. *Arab Crisis*, no. 26, 4 Sept. 1979. This was a weekly political magazine published in Sharjah.

23. On this topic, see al-Sayyid Muhammad Ibrahim, *Nationality in the United Arab Emirates: A Comparative Study of Nationality in the Gulf States*, Ministry of Information and Culture, UAE, 1978, p. 3.

24. Although there have been many studies of Arab and Asian immigration to the Gulf region, statistics stop at 1975, or even earlier. See, for instance, the group of studies on Arab and foreign immigration to the countries of the Gulf in the *Gulf Journal*, vol. 11, 1979, no. 2. This is a biannual scholarly journal which deals with the affairs of the Gulf and the Arabian peninsula, published by the Centre for Gulf Studies, University of Basra.

25. *Arab Crisis*, no. 9.

26. Ibid., no. 20.

27. *Arab Crisis*, no. 29, 26 Sept. 1978.

28. Na'ma Saqr, 'Federalism in the United Arab Emirates', paper presented at the Colloquium on Economic and Social Development Strategies in the Gulf, Exeter (UK), 9–13 July 1979, p. 13.

29. For the text of the document and reactions to it see *al-Ittihad*, Abu Dhabi, 20 March 1979.

30. Ghanim and al-Sha'ir, *National Strategy of the United Arab Emirates*, p. 88.

31. Timothy S. Niblock, 'The Possibilities for Unity in the Gulf', paper

presented at the Colloquium on Economic and Social Development Strategies in the Gulf, Exeter (UK), 9–13 July 1979, p. 26.

Chapter 5

1. See the charter of the Gulf Co-operation Council, published in the Kuwaiti press on 5 February 1981. The GCC includes the UAE, Bahrain, Saudi Arabia, Oman, Qatar, and Kuwait.

2. Urfan al-Shafi'i and Hazim al-Balawi, 'The Strategic Options for Development in Kuwait', paper presented at the Conference on Strategies and Policies for Industrialization in Kuwait, Kuwait, 24–26 March 1980.

3. There is a great deal of literature criticizing Arab co-operation and the ways it falls short of the aspirations of the Arab peoples. See, for example, the document produced by the University of Baghdad, 'Aspects of the Social and Economic Development of the Countries of the Gulf', and presented at the Colloquium for Economic and Social Development in the Gulf, Baghdad, Feb. 1980, pp. 167–98.

4. Najib Isa, *The Development Model in Gulf and Arab Economic Integration*, Beirut 1976, p. 116.

5. For a study of these bilateral agreements, see *Documents Relating to the Gulf and the Arabian Peninsula*, 1975, publications of the *Journal of Gulf and Peninsula Studies*, Kuwait 1979.

6. *Al-Qabas*, Kuwait, 7 Jan. 1981.

7. For a complete list of such companies, see the page devoted to Gulf share prices in any daily Kuwaiti newspaper. The number itself is taken from *al-Qabas*.

8. For a discussion of the legal arguments, see the two articles by Uthman Abd al-Malik in *al-Watan*, Kuwait, 20. Nov. 1979 and 3 Dec. 1979, and the two articles by Adil al-Tabataba'i in *al-Watan*, 17 Nov. 1979 and 24 Nov. 1979.

9. Regarding this question, it is reported that Ahmad al-Siwaidi, the former minister of foreign affairs, remarked, 'It is, indeed, odd that we were united by the Anglo-Indian rupee, but are divided by the Arab dirham and dinar.'

10. See Kuwaiti Law no. 33 for 1975, granting citizens of Saudi Arabia, Bahrain, and the UAE rights similar to those enjoyed by citizens of Kuwait.

11. See the editorial in the *Journal for Industrial Co-operation in the Gulf*, vol. 1, no. 2, Oct. 1980.

Chapter 6

1. J. S. Birks and C. A. Sinclair, *Arab Manpower—The Crisis of*

Development, London 1980, p. 160.

2. Ibid., p. 10.

3. Ibid., p. 16.

4. J. S. Birks and C. A. Sinclair, 'The Domestic Political Economy and Development of Saudi Arabia', paper presented at the Second Colloquium on the Gulf, Exeter (UK), 9 July 1980, p. 16.

5. Nadir Gharjani, 'Migrant Labour', *The Arab Future*, no. 23, Jan. 1981, p. 56.

6. Report of the Society for the Abolition of Slavery and the Protection of Human Rights, January 1981.

7. Rashid al-Rashid, 'Lecture on the Gulf Co-operation Council', *al-Anba*, Kuwaiti daily newspaper, 16 May 1981.

8. *Al-Nahar*, Beirut daily, 23 May 1981.

9. *Al-Jazirah*, 25 May 1981.

10. See the statement issued by the Communist and Workers' Parties in the Arab countries, *The Arab Left*, Paris, June 1981.

Chapter 7

1. Certain traditional circles claimed that even the writing of poetry was ritually impure and satanically inspired. Some poets became convinced of this and destroyed their work—for instance Abd al-Rahman al-Khalifi (Qatar, 1890–1943), who burned all his poetry before he died.

2. For details of these and previous statistics see 'Higher Education and Development in the Gulf States', paper presented at the Gulf States Arab Education Office, First Colloquium of Chancellors and Vice-Chancellors of Gulf Universities, Bahrain, 4–7 Jan. 1982.

3. Muhammad Mahmoud Shakir, 'The Decadence of Our Literary Life', *The Arab*, no. 184, vol. 82, p. 20. (Dunlop was Adviser to the Egyptian Ministry of Education.)

4. Quoted by Muhammad Safar, deputy minister for artistic affairs in the Ministry of Higher Education, Saudi Arabia, at the First Colloquium of Chancellors and Vice-Chancellors of Gulf Universities, Bahrain, 4–7 Jan. 1982.

5. Hussein Abd al-Hamid, Abu Shanab, 'The Role of Television in Creating a Balanced Arab Culture in the Gulf', unpublished MA dissertation.

Chapter 8

1. Nasif Abd al-Khaliq, 'The Role of Kuwaiti Women in the Management of Development', paper presented at the Second Regional Conference

on Women in the Gulf and the Arabian Peninsula, Kuwait, March 1981.

2. See, for instance, Lois Beck and Nikki Keddie, *Women in the Muslim World*, 2nd edn, Cambridge, Mass. 1979, p. 16.

3. Kamla Nath, 'Education and Employment among Kuwaiti Women', in Beck and Keddie, *Women in the Muslim World*, p. 181.

4. Samira Ibrahim Salam, 'A Study of the Reasons for Withdrawal from the Faculty of Medicine by Saudi Women Students', paper presented at the Second Regional Conference on Women in the Gulf and the Arabian Peninsula, Kuwait, March 1981.

5. The terms *asil* and *baisari* are quite common in the Gulf countries. An *asil* is a person descended from a well-known tribe or family. A *baisari* is a person whose pedigree is unestablished. This division is fundamentally economic in origin, since tribes that owned camels were generally considered more worthy of 'respect' than those that raised livestock or engaged in agriculture. For further details, see Muhammad Ghanim al-Rumaihi, *Oil and Social Change in Contemporary Gulf Societies*, Kuwait 1976.

6. In this context, *hijab* refers not only to the garment that covers the hair, but also to the long, flowing, ankle-length robes. Some people insist that the face and the feet also be covered.

7. Haidar Ibrahim Ali, 'The Incorporation of Women into the Development Plan: Problems and Possibilities', paper presented at the Second Regional Conference on Women in the Gulf and the Arabian Peninsula, Kuwait, March 1981, p. 54. The author's remarks are merely impressionistic, but the problem is real nevertheless.

8. Aliya Hussein, 'Employment and the Divorced Woman in Kuwait', paper presented at the Second Regional Conference on Women in the Gulf and the Arabian Peninsula, Kuwait, March 1981, p. 7. Although this is only a prelimary study, the author has been able to provide genuinely new insights into the socio-economic backgrounds of divorced men and women.

9. Linda Usra Soffan, *The Women of the Arab Emirates*, London 1980, p. 19.

10. Uthman Abd al-Malik, 'The Rights of Gulf Women and Personal Law', in *The Position of Women in Kuwait and the Gulf*, p. 78.

11. Ibid., p. 132.

12. Soffan, *Women of the Arab Emirates*, p. 81.

13. Kingdom of Saudi Arabia, General Secretariat for Girls, 'A Comprehensive Report on the Progress of Educational Activities in the Sphere of Girls' Education in the Kingdom over the Past Twenty Years' (subsequently referred to as the Education Report).

14. Ibid., p. 3.

15. This was in 1973. See Minority Rights Group report no. 27, *Arab Women*, London 1975, p. 13.

Chapter 9

1. For a detailed discussion of this point, see May al-Daftari, 'The

Problem of Workers in Kuwait and Qatar', *Journal of Gulf and Peninsula Studies*, vol. 6, no. 23, July 10, pp. 67–108.

2. J. S. Birks and C. A. Sinclair, 'Economic and Social Implications of Current Development in the Arab Gulf', paper presented at the Second Conference on Development in the Arabian Peninsula, Exeter (UK), 1980.

3. Ibrahim al-Ibrahim, *Arab Immigrant Workers and Social Development in the Gulf*, p. 80.

Chapter 10

1. This was true even of countries like Bahrain and Oman which produce little oil themselves. It has been estimated that 90 per cent of Oman's national income comes from oil and aid from the oil-producing countries. See John Townsend, *Oman: The Making of a Modern State*, London 1977, p. 18.

2. Ali Khalifa al-Kawari, 'The Nature of Socio-Economic Development', paper presented at the Second Regional Conference on Women in the Gulf and the Arabian Peninsula, Kuwait, March 1981.

3. See the article by Ghazi al-Qusaibi in the newspaper *al-Sharq al-Awsat*, 10 March 1980.

Index